DOG
SPIRIT

DOG SPIRIT

HOUNDS, HOWLINGS, AND HOCUS POCUS

PATRICIA TELESCO

Destiny Books
Rochester, Vermont

Destiny Books
One Park Street
Rochester, Vermont 05767
www.InnerTraditions.com

Destiny Books is a division of Inner Traditions International

LIBRARY OF CONGRESS CATALOGING-IN-PUBLICATION DATA
Telesco, Patricia.
    Dog spirit : hounds, howlings, and hocus pocus / Patricia Telesco.
        p. cm.
    Includes bibliographical references (p.).
    ISBN 0-89281-806-9 (alk. paper)
    1. Dogs—Miscellanea. 2. Dogs—Mythology. 3. Magic. I. Title.
    BF1623.A55 T45 2000
    398'.3699772—dc21   00-026000

Printed and bound in Italy

10 9 8 7 6 5 4 3 2 1

Text design and layout by Kristin Camp
This book was typeset in Minion with Trajan as the display typeface

Frontispiece: Joan Miró, *Dog Barking at the Moon* (Philadelphia
    Museum of Art). ©2000 Artists Rights Society (ARS), New
    York / ADAGP, Paris.
Page 6: Thomas Gainsborough, detail from *Mr. and Mrs. Andrews*
    (National Gallery, London)
Page 7 (top): Diego Velázquez, detail from *Las Meninas* (Museo del
    Prado, Madrid).
Page 7 (bottom): Jan Steen, detail from *The Family of Cats*
    (Szépmüvészeti Museum).

CONTENTS

ACKNOWLEDGMENTS

Thanks to Esther for helping me find reliable Web sites about dogs, and for her contagious enthusiasm for this subject.

Additional gratitude goes to Sirona for connecting me with Inner Traditions International, and to Dorothy for sharing her insights into the world of dogs.

Lynndee LeBeau, Coyote Winds *(Vashon Island)*.

*Everyone needs a spiritual guide, a minister, rabbi
counselor, wise friend, or therapist.
My own wise friend is my dog.*
GARY KOWALSKI
THE SOUL OF ANIMALS

INTRODUCTION

His faithful dog shall bear him company.
ALEXANDER POPE

The word *animal* comes from a Latin term meaning
"having a soul," and anyone who has ever owned a
dog will certainly agree that canines are among the
most personable and soulful of domesticated animals.
In our earliest natural encounters, we may have met with
the wild dogs that followed tribes to clean up any remnant
food. Over time, these dogs chose to live near people, slowly
becoming domesticated and eventually serving as

valued companions and helpmates to both tribes and individuals.

As the relationship between the two species developed, dogs started nudging their way into religion, literature, art, and nearly every other aspect of human society. Egyptians worshiped the dog in the form of the god Anubis, who accompanied souls safely to the afterlife. A fitting job for man's best friend! Greeks depicted the three-headed Cerberus guarding the entry to the underworld, and Artemis, Greek goddess of the hunt, had dog companions.

Homer wrote about dog's interactions with other animals in his stories of Ulysses, and Romans considered the dog a symbol of courage. In China dog statues were used for good luck and as protective talismans, and training dogs was a valued profession. On a more practical level, sheepdogs tended their flocks in Scotland, dogs raced and hunted in Arabia, and shipboard dogs took to the sea in Wales!

Today, dogs show up in casual conversation all the time. For example, if you're not "dog-tired" after a long day's work, you could still be overcome during summer's "dog days" and find yourself panting like a dog, or exclaiming, "Doggone it!" When someone is a good friend, he or she is "faithful as a dog," when we mark our place in a beloved book it becomes "dog-eared," and when there's a problem at home the individual in question finds him- or herself in the "doghouse"!

Not only have canines entered our culture via the spoken word, they've also made their mark in our books, entertainment industry, and daily life. Authors such as Jack London wrote about the unique and interesting relationships between dogs and humans. The entertainment industry continues to be enamored of dogs (*101 Dalmations* tops the list). In Alaska, dogsled racing is still a popular sport. Today, nothing could be more unique than the relationships dogs have as companions and helpers to physically challenged people.

Besides all this dogmatic doggerel, an entire industry has grown around these household pets. Dog collars were invented centuries ago and continue to be produced today; some are even studded with jewels. Toys, beds, treats, and hundreds of other dog accessories are sold everywhere from the neighborhood supermarket to the Internet, and there are literally thousands of dog breeders and dog fancier groups around the world. It's estimated that at least six thousand books have been written about dogs, and that 37 percent of American households shelter at least one dog.

What is it about this animal that has fascinated humans and endeared it to the hearts of so many? Certainly the devoted nature of the dog ranks among its highest attributes. Unlike independent cats, dogs seem to revel in cooperative relationships, and show gratitude for their domestic bliss.

Whatever the case, people in ancient and modern times have looked to dogs as important symbols, harbingers, helpmates, and housemates. The purpose of this book is to explore dogs in all of their guises, from their role in our human world and their participation in some of our greatest legends, to their ability as sensitives that recognize moments when the supernatural world touches our own.

While this exploration centers mostly on the domestic dog, other canines wander in and out of these pages as well. Foxes, dingos, African wild dogs, coyotes, wolves, and jackals are all close relatives of our household pets. The beliefs and stories surrounding domestic dogs cannot randomly be separated from those of their wild cousins.

Likewise, this book reviews mythical dogs such as the fairy dogs of Scotland; T'ien Kou, the fiery celestial dog of China; and the symbolic dogs that appear in carvings and paintings, in the coats of arms of families such as the Foxhounds, and even in modern logos. This study reveals much about dogs as an important archetype in human awareness.

Finally, for those ardent dog lovers who are lost without a dog at their heel, this book includes a chapter on choosing, understanding, and caring for a dog in natural, earth-friendly ways. I myself am a dog lover, having lived with at least one dog throughout my life.

Even if you're not a dog owner you may still find this exploration of the dog to be fun and interesting, filled with snappy tidbits of information from history, lore, and the everyday lives of these important animals. You may never look at dogs the same way again.

Cave Canem
A CARVING FOUND IN POMPEII,
MEANING "BEWARE THE DOG."

ONE
DOG DAYS

Next to man, there is no living creature
whose memory is so retentive.
PLINY THE ELDER

An old story claims that after humankind was created God saw our fragility and gave us dogs as
helpmates to overcome our shortcomings. Other tales
seem to mirror this idea, that somehow the dog was pri-
mordial—that dogs knew how to hunt, make fire, and
maintain their communion with the divine long before
we did. So, with God and his or her dog witnessing all

Mimbres bowl. The human figure is holding a staff from which hang a dog and a fish (used courtesy of the Peabody Museum of Archaeology and Ethnology, Harvard University).

we find the familiar faces of the coyote, jackal, hyena, and wolf. All of these creatures had the unique teeth we associate with dogs (the canine), long skulls, strong back legs, and insulating fur.

As humans slowly evolved away from transient groups into established villages about twelve thousand years ago, canines followed in tribal communities of their own, looking for food. In fact, the dog's ability to work cooperatively with other dogs is partly the reason for its survival. As wolves in particular stayed near human communities that favored a small, more social creature, some developed a rapport with humans. They became *Canis familiaris*—guard dogs, hunting dogs, and scavenger dogs who cleaned up the human garbage that might otherwise have drawn predators. The relationship between humans and dogs continued to develop.

The domestication process has somewhat altered today's dogs from the earliest fossils classified as *Canis familiaris*. The teeth and digestive systems of domestic dogs are still those of meat-eating hunters, they still communicate using their tails and sense of smell, and they still have excellent hearing. However today there is an increased interaction and camaraderie between humans and dogs. In addition dogs today have increased reproductive capacity and show greater variations in breed, size, fur length, and color.

There is evidence to suggest that domesticated dogs came into the picture at around the same time as domesticated livestock. This possibility is most strongly indicated by rock art in Asia, Turkey, and England depicting people going on what appear to be ritual hunts with creatures that look like dogs. And as for archaeological evidence, the skeletal remains of a creature considered to be a domesticated dog were found in Iraq; these remains date to 6600 B.C.E.

A limestone carving from approximately 1900 B.C.E. found in Thebes includes the image of a dog sitting dutifully at the feet of its family. This is purportedly Bouhaki, the first dog ever given a name. Alas, Egyptologists have argued over this interpretation for years, some believing the name actually belongs to a cat also pictured in the relief. So, the honor of the first named dog might then fall to another Egyptian depicted on a limestone stella from about 1600 B.C.E., Hemu-Ha. In Egyptian mythology, Ha was a desert god who defended against invaders—a suitable name for a faithful dog!

Horemheb kneeling in adoration before Anubis.

The Egyptians enjoyed their dogs nearly as much as they enjoyed their cats, and the penalty for killing a dog was death. These creatures were, in fact, considered partners in human life, from birth to death and everything between. Egyptians often mummified their pets and adorned the result with nearly as much jewelry as the

attended church with their families, were dressed like their masters, appeared in the circus, and, in the case of some guard dogs, even received wages for their services, often in the form of food.

The Spanish brought dogs with them to the New World, but these creatures were often ordered by their masters to brutally attack natives. Back in the Old World, some dogs were regarded as witch's familiars. Be that as it may, the love humans felt toward their dogs continued, evidenced in the eighteenth century by the frequent appearance of dogs in books, magazines, art, and even museum exhibits that drew huge crowds.

The prevalence of dog shows and breeding as an art form increased in the late 1800s, including the introduction of Eastern dogs. Unfortunately, alongside this growth came puppy mills and some other forms of abuse, which encouraged the creation of the SPCA (Society for the Prevention of Cruelty to Animals).

This, in turn, helped promote proper veterinary care for dogs and an emphasis on population control that remains to this day.

There are presently over four hundred breeds of dogs and over fifty million pet dogs in the United States alone, and the industry associated with these animals shows no signs of slowing down. In 1993 U.S. dog owners paid over $15 billion dollars to care for their dogs in a suitable manner, spending money on

everything from high-quality dog food to veterinary care to funerals. Should you wish it, you can even find a massage therapist for your dog, or a puppy psychiatrist!

Raining Cats and Dogs, *a nineteenth-century engraving.*

DOG CHRONICLES

Dogs have participated in human culture in ways one might not expect. For example, the popular expression "it's raining cats and dogs" originated in the seventeenth century when cats hunted on

from the prisons where their masters were kept. The dogs did not gobble down the food themselves, but took it to the slaves!

- Eighteen hundred years ago ancestors of today's greyhound entertained race crowds in Rome.
- The Bible contains over thirty references to dogs.
- Sometime between 495 C.E. and 1345 the Order of the Dog was established in France to honor knights who showed outstanding bravery and vigilance. This order was marked by a collar and a medallion featuring a dog. (The uncertainty about the date has to do with an argument over exactly who founded the "official" order.)

Study of a dog from da Vinci's sketchbook.

- In the 1300s Marco Polo returned to Europe with tales of Asian hunting packs numbering over five thousand hounds. This helped spur an interest in hunting as a sport that spread throughout Europe, and eventually reached England.
- During the sixteenth century, St. Christopher became strongly associated with dogs because of his faithful nature, and was sometimes even described as being dog-headed.
- When caught in a violent storm at sea, King James II of England was quoted as shouting, "Save my dogs!"
- In the late 1600s the Netherlands became the first region to outlaw dogfights.
- Leonardo da Vinci boasted among his other great works a complete collection of anatomical dog studies.

- In 1750 the first St. Bernards became guide dogs to monks living in snowy climes. This eventually led to their use in avalanche rescue operations.
- In the late 1700s, Pennsylvania Lieutenant Governor Penn proposed that each soldier be allotted three shillings per month to care for a dog because they could help uncover enemy strongholds.
- Queen Victoria was adored by many people in part because of her fondness for dogs. Her favorites appeared to have been collies, one of which took meals with her.
- England's first dog show was organized in 1859.
- The first commercially made dog biscuit came to market in 1860.
- In the late 1800s the first competitive dogsled races were held in Alaska.
- In 1899 feminist Marguerite Durand founded the first public dog cemetery in Paris.
- Elizabeth Browning almost didn't marry Robert because he hated her dog. Despite this, her cocker spaniel got to go along with them on the honeymoon!
- At the outset of World War I Germany and her allies began a nationwide search for dog handlers in order to enlist thousands of dogs in the war. The United States followed up this idea in the 1940s with the formation of the K-9 Corps.
- At the end of World War I, Germany began using guide dogs to help injured vets. Formalized training programs for guide dogs now exist throughout the United Sates, Europe, and many other countries.

the threshold of your home. To foster devotion in a relationship, both people might carry the pattern of the constellation Canis Major with them on paper, a piece of jewelry, or other item especially designed with love and commitment in mind.

Ahuizol: A Mexican fantastic beast that was a cross between a dog and a monkey, it was predominantly a trickster figure, with a hand on the end of its tail to catch people unaware.

Amarock: In Eskimo tradition this is a giant wolf and a heroic figure in their legends. In his wolf form he represents courage and the ability to find your way through the wilderness using keen instincts.

Black dog: In Scotland, Ireland, and parts of England this is a ghostly dog that represents an ill omen, or who protects graveyards from demonic forces. With this in mind, the image of a black dog could be used for safeguarding precious items, or carried as a talisman to help recognize nature's signs when they come.

Bush dog: A smaller wild dog that looks slightly bearish, the bush dog communicates with its fellows by whining. Group contact is very important to this animal, making it a symbol of kinship and community.

Calygreyhound: As the name implies, this heraldic creature

Nootka wooden mask, used in the Wolf Dance.

represents swiftness. It has the body of an antelope, talons of an eagle, and the hindlegs of the greyhound.

Canis Major and Canis Minor: These constellations represent faithful dogs. Canis Major houses Sirius, known as the Dog Star and named for Orion's favorite hunting dog, now accompanying him across the heavens. These star patterns might be used on any item designed to foster dedication, good instincts, or the ability to "sniff" out the truth.

Cephus: The Egyptians in Memphis worshiped this creature, likely because of its strength and tenacity, which is signified by a satyr head atop the body of a dog-bear.

Coyote: Both a trickster and a hero, the coyote is a medicine dog filled with magic and humor. In the tarot his card is the Fool because coyotes depend on their ability to get out of self-inflicted situations using clever phrases, a naive appeal, and subterfuge. He symbolizes an odd dichotomy of quick wittedness and roguishness. Generally the coyote might be best used in items devised for thinking on one's feet, improving communication skills, or augmenting your sense of humor.

Cu Sith: A Scottish fairy dog who is known for its silent movement. This creature is described as being large and greenish, which is how it should be illustrated for any magic intended to decrease one's visibility in a situation.

Dhole: A relative of the dog that hunts during the day using a keen sense of smell, this creature represents the ability to allow instinct to guide you toward success, and away from trouble.

Dingo: In Australia this creature is regarded as having a soul

Aboriginal sculpture (Australian Institute of Aboriginal Studies).

to symbolize service, vigilance, and unwavering devotion.

Dog spirit: Embodied by the Dog Star in China, this spirit is said to control family fate through celestial movements. To invoke its power in changing your destiny, make a pattern of Canis Major on a stone or paper, and carry it with you regularly. (Try holding it when reading your horoscope!)

Fox: The power of cunning, guile, and quick decision making, for boon and bane, are some of this creature's attributes. In the shamanic sense, the fox also has strong associations with the power of shape-shifting and illusion. This association may have developed because foxes tend to live in in-between places (the meeting grounds between the worlds), such as the border between forest and glade.

If properly appeased, the fox spirit will bring luck, or bear messages between the worlds. Several Native American medicine people call on the fox spirit to help with healing. Persians relied on the fox to guide souls to the afterlife, and the fox is an important totem in a variety of cultural settings. With

Anubis guarding Tutankhamen's tomb (Griffith Institute, Oxford).

this in mind, the image of a fox is an excellent focus for meditations that open your spiritual awareness to other realms, or to the human aura through which so much healing takes place.

As an interesting aside, the phenomenon of will-o'-the-wisp is sometimes called "fox fire" because of its elusiveness, and Scandinavians nicknamed the aurora borealis "fox light" because it constantly shifts and changes.

Funerary dogs: When depicted as part of death rites, a dog symbolizes human fidelity, love, faithfulness, and courage. Alternatively, when the image appeared on a headstone it may have been used to safeguard the body and soul of the deceased.

Garm: A huge, monstrous dog of Celtic tradition, Garm is said to have guarded the entrance to the underworld until he tried to get the underworld to revolt, resulting in his death.

Hyena: Because it is a scavenger, the symbolism of the hyena is nearly universally negative. Aristotle, for example, claimed the creature tried to mimic the human voice to lure people to their deaths. Far Eastern people think this creature is a reincarnated wizard, and in Arabia evil wizards are said to assume this animal's form.

Today the hyena is known for its laughter, but still has negative connotations, so I wouldn't suggest using this as a positive

symbol. But you might ritually destroy a picture of a hyena when trying to dissipate gossip or mockery.

Jackal: In Bantu mythology the jackal was once a brother to the dog until the dog chose human companionship over that of other animals. This torn alliance may be why many cultures associate the jackal with misdeeds or malice.

One notable exception exists. Egyptians see the jackal as a helpful creature that guides souls between the worlds. In this context, jackal images might be good for magic aimed at creat-

The Ascetic Jackal and His Brothers, *from the* Kalila Wa Dimna.

ing opportunity or finding one's way.

Lion dog: A Buddhist composite creature that defends the spirit and letter of the law, the lion dog also represents the universe's duality and the balance that is necessary in all things. The lion dog image provides excellent focus for inspiring symmetry and an understanding of universal truths.

Mimic dog: This creature, which may not have been a dog at all, purportedly lived in ancient Egypt. It is described as having the face of a hedgehog and the body of a monkey. Historians such as Ptolemy report that this animal was able to mimic anyone or anything with amazing accuracy, and acted as a servant in more prominent households. This might give rise to using an image of the mimic dog to empower sympathetic and imitative magic.

Puppy: Exactly how puppies came to represent ego or narcissism is uncertain, but a clue might be found in the phrase "puppy-dog eyes," which describes the look we give to get what we want—a function of ego. We know that Romans often offered pups to the gods to protect their crops from mildew, but the connection between that and contemporary symbolism has been lost to history.

p002c

Qiqlon: In Inuit tradition Qiqlon is a much feared hairless dog that as a spirit can cause seizures. To avoid being stricken, one need only speak its name. (This protective measure is often used with malevolent spirits; people once trusted heavily the power of names.)

Sea-dog: This is a composite creature from heraldry, depicted with a dog's face, webbed feet, scales, and a beaverlike tail. I suspect this creature was less symbolic in nature, and used instead to combine the imagery from several households under one banner. Nonetheless, it might be useful in mystical procedures where the powers of water and earth are necessary for success.

T'ien Kou: A red dog of Chinese lore who lives in the stars, this creature can be very tenacious, guarding us from evil influences. For whatever reason, T'ien Kou seems more effective as a household protector than a portable amulet. Keep his watchful gaze turned outward to see any forthcoming dangers.

Werewolf: The word *lycanthropy* comes from *lycos* meaning "wolf." Nonetheless a werewolf may be a wolf, hyena, or fox. The concept of human-to-animal transformation probably arose out of shamanic shape-shifting rites and imitative magic. Be that as it may, myths of werewolves dot the globe, with transformations being driven by the moon or by the psychic powers of a sorcerer.

For most contemporary practitioners the werewolf strongly reminds us of our wild nature and our connection with the animal kingdom. In this sense, it is a symbol that could be positively reclaimed for effective shape-shifting and earth healing rites.

Wolf: The quality generally associated with the wolf is evil. Yet, this probably has more to do with the creature's association with gods and goddesses who guard the gates to the underworld than its actual traits. In addition, the various wolf cults that have appeared throughout history usually had rather distasteful, frightening rites. And we all know the phrase "a wolf in sheep's clothing" represents the ultimate in deceit.

Be that as it may, the wolf was sacred to Ares, Silvanus, Mars, and Romulus and Remus. In fact, the wolf is a symbol for Rome. Irish legends tell of some helpful wolves with doglike character-

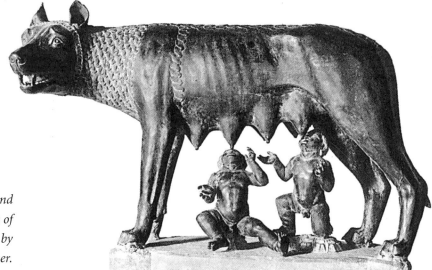

Statue of Romulus and Remus, the founders of Rome, being suckled by their wolf-mother.

istics, and many Celtic deities had wolves for pets, or could shape-shift into a wolf. For example, Cernunnos, the horned god who represents our link to nature, had a wolf companion.

Norse tradition shows Odin riding a wolf, but also has Fenris, a wolf created by Loki, as a destroyer. Valkyries ride wolves across the sky when seeking out slain heros. The disparate symbolism appears again, however, as wolves try to eat the sun to capture its power.

In the Far East the wolf is revered for its agility, strength, and perseverance. Among Native Americans the wolf is a teacher—one who can guide us on our path and help us discover the psychic self. Therefore, mystical methods aimed at improving intuitive ability, learning, tenacity, and staying on track are probably the four best applications for wolf symbolism.

The animals, afraid for their lives, returned to the forest—except for the dog who, after careful thought, jumped over the rift and stayed with humans.
NATIVE AMERICAN STORY

TWO

DOGGEREL

The Dog was at creation and saw it first. God said so.
OLD APHORISM

Folklore embraces communal ideas about life and its numerous mundane, ethical, or spiritual questions. Most folklore began as moralistic stories that were then passed down familial or cultural lines through oral tradition. Among the literally thousands of folktales and their variations, the symbolic value of dogs for teaching and illustrating important lessons is not overlooked.

For example, the most popular of the Native American folktales is about a young woman who takes a lover. Unknown to her, this man is a dog during the day and a man by night. Many months later she gives birth to pups, and her tribe deserts her. The great spirit Crow comes to the young woman's aid, helping her hide the children and giving fire for the hearth. The woman destroys the babies' dog-skins, making them human.

Now, because the children are part dog, they grow up to become wonderful hunters. Whenever Crow spirit visits, he receives meat in thanks for his assistance. Later, when the young woman's original tribe is starving, Crow tells them of the wonderful hunters, and the tribe returns to the woman, sheepish and embarrassed by their own lack of devotion and kindness.

Other Native American stories follow various motifs that emphasize the dog's attributes. In some tales a dog tracks down errant lovers, pointing out skill in tracking or its strong sense of smell. In others, a dog may plead to become humankind's companion on earth, highlighting its fidelity. Other stories still claim that dogs were once human, but eventually chose their present form to better serve humankind, exemplifying charity.

These are but few examples of the many wonderful dog tales kept alive by diligent bards. This chapter explores several more, and also the myths and legends that brought dogs and their relatives to storytime gatherings around the world.

THE FOLKLORE DOG

European folktales are littered with dogs, most of which are faithful companions to a heroic figure. Included in this massive list we find the Norse saga of Olaf Triggvason, and the English tale of King Arthur's dog, Cavall. In Welsh tradition, Prince Llewellyn had a hound named Gelert who died defending the prince's son from a wolf.

West Africa brings us a wonderful story about a faithful and loving dog who helps his master gain a wife. According to this story a young man fell helplessly in love with two beautiful girls. In the girls' village, however, one could marry only if one could

African nail dog. Each embedded object represents a prayer offered by the tribe (Zaire).

discover the young women's names. The young man went away terribly disappointed, but his dog stayed behind and listened diligently. As he followed the girls around, getting treats and water from them, he overheard their names. The dog dutifully brought this knowledge to his master, who happily took the girls for wives.

In this example, we can see that folklore tries to illustrate the dog's traits, specifically here the motif of a dog as a virtuous teacher. This particular theme appears frequently in many other stories.

The Fox Mate

A rather romantic folktale tells of a lonely man who lived in the woods. One day he came home to find the house in order and dinner made, but no sign of company. Over the next few days and nights he watched, and discovered to his surprise that a fox was coming into his house, removing its fur, and turning into a woman. The man, in an act of foxlike cunning, hid the fur and the couple lived happily for many years—that is until the woman rediscovered her fur and ran back to the wild! The lesson here is that one cannot force love or constrain it or it will not last.

The Jackal

In Asian folktales the lion keeps the jackal as a friend and ally. The jackal helps gather game for the lion, a task for which he is rewarded with leftovers. This mutual bond, however, has given rise to the idea that the jackal is cowardly because he will not kill his own food. To this day, in many regions where the jackal runs wild, eating the creature's flesh is taboo—eating the meat causes fearfulness and timidity. The only exception seems to be in northern Africa where the jackal is esteemed as wise and educated because it allows the lion to do the dirty work for it!

The Religious Wolf

An old story tells us that one day a wolf heard of the easy life in monasteries, specifically that there was little work to do and plenty of lamb for dinner. So, the wolf decided to become religious and entered the monastery. The monk told him he must learn to read and write in order to stay, and the wolf agreed. With much effort, the wolf learned A and B, but it was not easy. Finally, when the old monk pointed to C and asked what it stood for, the wolf, tired of learning and anxious for his reward, gleefully said, "LAMB!" Well, his true intentions were then discovered and he was returned to the forests.

Dissenting Dogs

As is true with most folklore, the dark side of the dog and his kin emerges in stories, too. Good illustrations of this dark side come from Aesop's fables. In one, a dog lies lazily atop a haystack in a manger. Each time a horse or ox tries to eat, it nips it. This story was written to illustrate selfishness or salaciousness—the dog would not give hay to the other animals even though the dog itself could not eat the hay! Aesop's fables also frequently use the fox to illustrate lessons. In *The Fox and the Grapes,* the fox shows us the very human trait of disdaining what one cannot get. In *The Fox and the Raven,* the fox uses flattery to get the raven's cheese, teaching us that flattery is not a friend.

Another example that disparages the fox comes from Japan where the *kitsune* (the fox) is a very magical animal that can charm people and shape-shift. All such creatures are generally regarded as evil (with the exception of the Inari fox, who represents the god of the rice harvest). This view of the fox as charmer and trickster is mirrored in Native American traditions with one important difference: Many of the fox's tricks are designed to teach important lessons to humans blinded by pride or vanity.

In Native American lore, coyotes share the fox's trickster reputation. My favorite tale is from the Hopi: Coyote created the Milky Way through his negligence. He took the lid off a pot, which then spilled into space. This particular story illustrates another important role that folklore fulfills, that of explaining natural phenomena, as the next three stories show.

JON GRaHAM

A dissenting dog's view of French political life (graffiti on the wall is a symbol for the right-wing National Front party), Paris, 1977.

In the Doghouse

An Irish tale explains why many cats live in the house while their dog companions stay outside. Apparently the dog and cat argued over this point for some time until at last their master set up a race. The animal that won would get the spot by the fire, while the other would house itself outdoors. Unfortunately for the dog a beggar watching the race thought the dog was going to bite him, and struck the creature as it ran by. The cat won the race.

Catch that Cat!

Ever wonder why dogs chase cats? A Yiddish folktale tells us that at one time cats safeguarded a royal decree that forbade people from bothering dogs. After some time, the law enforcers forgot about the decree and tried to round up the dogs. Unfortunately, when the dogs tried to retrieve the paperwork from the cats' lair, it was found nibbled to bits by mice. Upon discovering this, the cats began chasing mice, and the dogs chased after the cats, and so it has remained to this day.

Kangra School, detail from The White Kali *(Archaeological Survey of India, New Dehli)*

A Dog and His Bone

Haitian folklore reveals why dogs can't resist bones. Apparently the dog and cat had differing opinions on whether animals should live forever. The cat felt they should not. After a long argument, they agreed to consult their god and request a decision. Both creatures bathed and readied themselves and headed toward the god's house. Along the way the dog came across a bone, and his nose would not let him pass it by. So the cat arrived at god's house first, animals became transitory, and the dog to this day cannot pass up a good bone.

PSYCHIC POOCH?

And, for those of us who believe dogs can see spiritual beings, a Japanese folktale agrees. The story goes that a man visited the land of the dead to find it looking much like his village, but no one there could see or hear him. No one, that is, except for the dogs, who barked when he appeared.

Another story from Rome mirrors this concept with a neat twist. In this case a man's dead wife appeared to him as an angry ghost, begging him to burn the last of her clothing so she could rest in peace. He implored her to tell him what had not yet been burned, but at that fateful moment the man's dog began barking, apparently at the ghost, and she vanished. The master was very angry, and was just about to punish the dog when he saw the real reason for the creature's noise. Next to the dog lay a single sandal, the wife's last remaining item of clothing. He immediately burned the sandal, and the woman's spirit never returned.

Hokusai (1760–1849),
The Kokka.

TREASURE DOGS

A French moralistic tale recounts the unique way in which a young man named Atis achieved happiness. Apparently Atis fell madly in love with a young maiden named Argia, and enlisted

the aid of a fairy to win her. The fairy transformed into a spaniel and made Atis into a dirty beggar. When they arrived in Argia's hometown and she saw them, she loved the tricks that the little dog performed, so much so that she said she would pay any price to make the dog her own. The beggar refused at first, rubbing the dog's paw, which subsequently released gems and coins. "See," he said, "my dog is very valuable, and if you would have him, you must take me as well!" Argia accepted, and immediately Atis returned to his normal handsome, young self, making everyone happy. So it is that we learn two lessons: good things come in small packages, and what you see is not always what you get!

MYTHICAL DOGS

Myths and folktales are sometimes difficult to differentiate because each of them have implausible elements. What sets myths apart is that the story tells of a creature, person, or item believed to have once existed, although there is little historical evidence to support this claim. By comparison, a folktale is often specifically devised as an exaggeration to illustrate a point.

A good example of a mythical dog may be seen in the Mimic dog of Egypt. Purportedly this "dog" bore the head of a hedgehog and the body of an ape. Writings place the Mimic as living during the time of Ptolemy, and ascribe to it amazing mimicry talents. Because of this skill, the creature became a servant in wealthy households.

Another good illustration of mythical dogs can be given by

its relative, the fox. In both China and Japan, myths are filled with shape-shifting humans that turn into foxes and prance merrily through the fields. Many of these stories indicate a belief that either the shape-shifter is actually a descendent of the fox, or that the fox through the acquisition of power appears as a human. Interestingly enough, the latter is able to become an immortal and even a god!

WOLVES AND WEREWOLVES

Among the woodland tribes of North America, the wolf plays an important role in mythology as the brother of a great hero named Nana Bozho who rules over the land of the dead. Here and in other settings the wolf and the coyote are also considered brothers who travel together, the wolf helping to organize human social groups and teaching rituals.

A witch turned werewolf attacks travelers. From von Kaysersberg's Die Emeis, *1517.*

Perhaps the most widely known wolf myth is that of the werewolf. While most people think of werewolves as European in origin, myths about shape-shifting humans are told around the world, and often include the wolf as the figure into which humans transform. Exactly what causes the transformation depends on the particular myth. In some, shape-shifting is a curse, involuntarily triggered by lunar phases. In others it is a power evoked by donning a wolf's fur. Should the wearer forget to remove the fur at dawn, however, he could be trapped in the animal form. The widespread belief in the lycanthropic myth became so strong in sixteenth- and seventeenth-century Europe that some thirty thousand people suspected of being werewolves were killed.

Humans in Dog's Clothing?

Returning to the dog proper, a painting by Bernard Picard illustrates a dog myth. The image is one of an unnamed Oriental leader being handed a dog on his deathbed. Purportedly this scene was painted during a real event where the gentleman requested his dog's presence— not for comfort, but so that with his last breath he could release his spirit and his hunting talents into the dog! The concept of soul transference isn't as unique as you might think. In Africa, for example, it is believed that a murdered person can enter the body of a hyena to attack the one who caused the deadly injury.

Edward Hopper, detail from Cape Cod Evening *(National Gallery of Art).*

Dutiful Dogs

On the Aran Islands there is a myth about two collies who had been companions throughout life. The two resided in a butcher's house close to the ocean. One day the older of the two went to the water and drowned. When the other collie found him, she raced to the butcher's shop and grabbed a steak. She then returned to her friend and carefully placed the meat in the old dog's mouth so he would not want for food in the next life.

Dog Kings

The Norse tell a myth about a king named Eystein who had been temporarily sent out of his country. When he regained his power, he felt he could not trust his countrymen. He offered them a choice of rulers: his slave or his dog. The people chose the dog, since they knew a dog would not lie nor deceive humankind. This royal canine supposedly reigned for three years, making various decrees into law with but a paw print.

Dog Star

How and why did the Dog Star receive its name? According to Sumerian myths it is so designated because of its timely, devoted nature, akin to the dog's. The star appears exactly when the Nile rises, signaling the time to move the flocks, even as a sheepdog might signal the shepherd of impending troubles. It's interesting to note that far across the ocean in the New World, Native Americans associated this star with the coyote, who is also a water-bringer.

Moon Dogs

We know that the image of a dog baying at the moon appears in many stories and myths, but why? Well in Greek, Irish, and other mythologies, dogs are associated with lunar gods and goddesses, and in some cases with the magical lunar landscape of other-realms. In Ireland the next life is sometimes called Moonland, and its entryway is dutifully guarded by dogs who allow to go through only those spirits whose time has truly come. They also make sure a spirit doesn't accidentally wander off, never to find peace.

Dog Demigods

In Japan, Ti'en Kou is a celestial dog who descends from heaven and warns people of disaster. Myths tell us that the first time the creature appeared was about the sixth century B.C.E. Descriptions say he flew like a ball of fire, with yellow light shining from him in all directions. Shortly thereafter fields were blighted, and the dog remained in the skies. Locals purportedly tried to appease Ti'en Kou with liver, but the spirit remained until the danger had passed. From this myth evolved the practice of keeping an image of Ti'en Kou in homes as a protective spirit.

Fortunately Ti'en Kou's appearances seem to be rare. A Chinese historian from the second century B.C.E. described a dog who appeared like a shooting star, accompanied by thunder. The Chinese, however, have a special weapon to combat the fearful spirit. It is the duty of an immortal named Chang Hsien to shoot the creature using a bow of mulberry wood to fend off its attacks.

Chinese celestial dog-demon.

DOGS IN LEGEND

Legends vary from folklore in that they chronicle the lives of important people, events, or organizations, but the stories cannot be wholly authenticated. Generally in legends a fantastic element either reveals important characteristics about the legend's protagonist or teaches a lesson. In the Far East, for example,

4. Le Tsarévitch Ivan et le loup gris.

Contes Russes : Aquarelles de Zvorikine.

Т-во СКОРОПЕЧАТНИ А. А. ЛЕВЕНСОНЪ, МОСКВА.

legends claim that some of the greatest poets and philosophers benefited greatly from the fox. How? By caring for them during storms. The thunder god punishes fox spirits who obtain their power through improper means. Since scholars and great thinkers tend to be upright sorts, foxes who have reason to fear the god's wrath seek shelter with them. In return, as the fox spirit grows in power, he blesses the kindly humans with wealth and fame.

Here are some other interesting dog legends.

Opposite: Illustration from a nineteenth-century version of the popular Russian folktale of Tsaravitch Ivan and the Gray Wolf.

Faithful Dogs of Greece

Greek legends tell us that Pericles' father, Xanithippus, had a dog that swam by his side to Salamis when Athenians were forced to leave their city. Purportedly this dog was buried next to his master in a site still known as the "dog's grave" in Cynossema. It was also in this part of the world that Alexander the Great supposedly named the city Peritas to honor the memory of his loving, devoted dog.

Dog Detectives

In Brittany legend recounts how a greyhound helped locate the slain body of his master. Apparently King Apollo was killed by King Clovis's son, who desired Apollo's wife. The murderer tried to hide his victim, but the faithful greyhound followed the body of his master. The dog attempted to bury the body, and then lay beside it until both were discovered. It was none other than King Clovis who found the dog and the body and subsequently set

A Greek hunter with his dog.

about uncovering the culprit. It was finally determined that the king's son was to blame, and he was ordered to die by fire. Because of this legend, the dog remains a symbol of retribution and the law in action.

UNDERWORLD DOGS

The Norse, Celtic, Greek, and German stories of a famous person's death being preceded by the Hounds of the Wild Hunt are numerous. According to these legends, a god or goddess of the underworld comes to the earth with his or her hounds just prior to or immediately after death to collect the soul. One cannot elude the keen nose of these dogs, and to hear them is a very bad omen.

People who have reported Hunt sightings over the years speak of huge dogs with fiery eyes that pierce night's dark shroud as sure as the sun. They are always accompanied by a master or mistress on horseback, who disappears back into the mists along with the dogs once their task is complete.

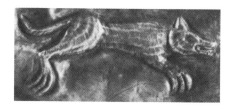

Detail from Gundestrup cauldron (Nationalmuseet, Copenhagen).

ANCESTRAL DOGS

In Irish lore King Cormac was said to have been suckled by wolves, and many other families claim descent from the creature. This is not surprising since the Celts picture many heroes with a wolf or dog companion. Similarly, many North American tribal cultures hold the wolf as an ancestral teacher and pathfinder who helps them return to Sirius, where the gods abide.

Religious Dogs

An English legend recounts a time when a dog helped create a new religious order. According to this tale, when the envoy for Henry VIII came to the pope to try to get a divorce from Catherine of Aragon, the envoy's faithful dog bit the pope's toe in an odd misunderstanding. Needless to say, the divorce was not granted. Consequently, Henry broke off his associations with Rome and created the Church of England.

Potpourri

And there's still more! Legends claim that Mary, Queen of Scots, had a Maltese under her skirts before her beheading; that aboard the *Titanic* a Newfoundland tried to warn his master of impending danger by barking and running in circles; and that a prophetic

dog appeared to St. Dominic's mother in a dream, which is why that order's colors are black and white and why they're called the "dogs of god"!

BREED BELIEFS

Folklore and legends each propose different explanations for how various breeds of dogs developed, why they have specific char acteristics, how the breed spread across the world, and what type of influence a dog of a particular breed has on its owner. Through such stories our ancestors resolved the mystery that we now recognize as caused by genetics, and the odd coincidences that occurred among owners of specific breeds. What follows here is a sampling of such beliefs, wives' tales, and observations from around the world.

Afghanhound: This dog apparently got its wet nose on Noah's Ark when it literally followed its nose. The canine used its pointed snout to plug holes in the ark so water wouldn't leak in!

Airedale: Some claim this dog has a propensity for learning human language, and once it does it can one-up the best conversationalist with its witty use of vocabulary.

Akita: Among the Japanese it is believed that the Akita is the result of a successful union between humans and dogs, and as such is deserving of special treatment. In fact, there was a long period in Japanese history during which only nobles could own

Opposite: Gustave Courbet, Bonjour Monsieur Courbet *(Museé Fabre, Montpelier).*

them. As an interesting aside, Hellen Keller is to be thanked for the introduction of this breed to the United States—she was given one by the Japanese government.

Basenji: In Africa this dog bears a nickname that means "jumping up and down," referring to how it moves through tall grass. Local legends say that the only way to keep track of this dog is by belling it—it moves far too fast for any human eye to follow. Additionally, the Basenji were the original fire-bringers, for which they were rewarded with eternal care and feeding by humankind.

François Boucher, detail from Diana Bathing *(Louvre).*

Basset hound: In India wild cousins of these dogs are left to wander undisturbed because they are thought to be of heavenly origin.

Beagle: While these dogs are good hunters, their reputation as great rabbit dogs was frequently built by storytellers. One in particular claims that even after being accidentally cut in half and put together backward, beagles so love hunting that they will adapt and catch rabbits anyway!

Bloodhound: In Celtic tradition, the summoner and collector of souls is always accompanied by these hounds who cannot be fooled, and refuse to give up the hunt until proper judgment is served. This may be why the baying of bloodhounds is considered an omen of death.

Borzi: Russian myths tell us that the progenitor of all modern Borzi was born on the hunt by a pregnant female trying to defend her mate. When the mother fell, two pups died but the third lived and became immortal.

Boston terrier: Of all breeds, these canines are said to have the highest rating for psychic ability, and the best capacity for remembering numbers and schedules.

Bulldog: Known for its gruff and tough demeanor, stories tell us that the way to a bulldog's heart is through its ears and eyes. If you want to make a bulldog your friend, don't show it any fear, sing it a song, and speak softly. Your courage and kindness will be rewarded with kinship.

Chihuahua: Mexican legends connect this dog with the god Xolotl, who guides souls to the other-realms. Apparently Xolotl appears with the head of a Chihuahua that has gems for eyes.

Chow: In Irish mythology, chows guard the secret magical hills that house fairy folk.

Collie: Of all the breeds, this one seems to have gained the reputation of being able to find its way home, no matter what, thanks to popular literature.

Coonhound: This dog was given huge ears by God to help it in the hunt. An old wives' tale claims that as the ears flop up and down they send air to the nose, and thereby provide the scent necessary for tracking. Such stories also say that these hounds are so smart, you have but to show them the size of the raccoon you want and they'll fetch it!

Corgi: In Welsh tradition, the corgi is a gift from the fairy

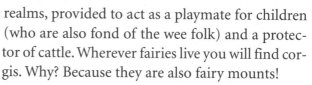

realms, provided to act as a playmate for children (who are also fond of the wee folk) and a protector of cattle. Wherever fairies live you will find corgis. Why? Because they are also fairy mounts!

Dachshund: Some people claim this dog is an ancestor of the god Anubis, the guide to the underworld and deliverer of souls. Why? Because of the dog's appearance and its love for digging in the earth, exploring caverns, and running through tunnels.

Dingo: In Australian mythology, two dingoes are responsible for creating the Magellanic Clouds, two conspicuous patches of light seen near the south celestial pole. After their death the two dogs rose into the sky, but had to stop and urinate on the way to heaven. This liquid formed the nebulae.

Doberman pinscher: The common myth about Dobermans is that they fear nothing, and will stand firm in the face of anything. This idea may have developed from the early Doberman's ferocity, which has been somewhat bred out.

Golden retriever: This breed is so dedicated to its human companions that it is believed that a golden will go beyond death's doorway to try and retrieve its master's spirit.

Great Dane: This breed is heralded as an odd cross between jester and king, having nobility and comedy all rolled into one furry package. Superstition tells us that if you hear this dog howl at what seems to be nothing, look quickly between its ears and the same spirit vision the Dane is having will appear to you. This wives' tale may have led to the development of Scooby-Doo, a

Opposite: Great Danes on a Brooklyn stoop.

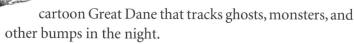

cartoon Great Dane that tracks ghosts, monsters, and other bumps in the night.

Greyhound: Irish stories are filled with examples of this dog's love of people. In one legend, Tristan gives Isolt his beloved dog. Tristan then leaves, but the dog refuses to run after him, simply hovering near his mistress as if his joy had disappeared.

Husky: In Eskimo tradition, this breed was born of either a raven's talons or wood, probably alluding to its tough and rugged physical nature. It is also said that God originally sent these dogs to humans to act as comforters and helpmates during times of grief.

Irish setter: Literature depicts setters as canines with tremendous love and courage that seems contagious to humans who own them. Additionally, Irish setters are said to have a quirky sense of humor, likely due to their playful demeanor.

Labrador retriever: The most popular belief about these limber, water-loving dogs is that one, the ancestor to many, belonged to Saint John.

Lhasa apso: Chinese myths say that this dog is the ancestor of the lion dog (see page 26), a semidivine creature who embodies the spirit of the law. Stories also tell that a Lhasa accompanied the Bodhidharma, a Buddhist patriarch. To own one brings luck.

Mastiff: Persian legends say that the mastiff won't fight anyone but a worthy opponent, specifically lions and elephants! This is especially interesting since in Greek mythology mastifflike dogs guard the gates of hell and guarded the baby Zeus.

Pekingese: In Japanese art, this dog is connected with Buddha. It is pictured as his dog-aspect, the Dog of Fo, which is very similar to the Lion Dog and the Chinese depictions of Lhasas.

Pit bull: Avid lovers of this breed claim it can size up any person's intention simply by observing his or her body language. These dogs are also considered very tough and durable, coming away from seemingly dire situations unscathed.

Pomeranian: Stories of this little dog are intertwined with those of fox dogs in various parts of the world. In northern areas such as Russia and Lapland many people consider themselves descendants of Pomeranians. In Europe these dogs were popular as wizards' familiars and shamans' companions because of their mythical spiritual power.

Poodle: English legends tell that Prince Rupert owned a white poodle who had tremendous magical powers. He could divine the future, find any concealed item, speak several different languages, and shape-shift at will.

Rhodesian Ridgeback: In African folktales, this dog's sorrowful song presages the death of its owner.

Rottweiler: Dogs bearing the image of the rottweiler appear regularly in Teutonic mythology, often as companions to important heroes or as the gods themselves, even Siegfried and Thor.

Saluki: In Arabia this is the only dog regarded as sacred and clean, because it was a gift from Allah to serve as a partner in the hunt. This belief may have arisen from a story in the Koran about a saluki that guarded seven young sleepers for over three hundred years and in so doing earned itself a place in paradise. (An interesting aside: this dog has been clocked running at speeds of up to 35 and 40 miles per hour.)

Samoyed: The way this breed was received often depended on cultural feelings about white dogs and what they represent. For example, in some parts of Europe seeing such a dog foretold death, while in Native American tradition a white dog bears messages to the spirit realms for us.

Shar-pei: In China some stories claim that this breed is actually descended from the crawling dragon of myth, whose feet point east, the direction of beginning and west, the place wherein the ancestors reside. Consequently, in this part of the world shar-peis symbolize strength.

Sheepdog: The favorite myth about this dog is that, despite the hair hanging over its eyes, it can always outwit and catch a hungry wolf with little fuss. In Christian writings, a priest or minister is sometimes allegorically referred to as a sheepdog because he guards the figurative "flock." The Bible tells us that a sheepdog preserved Abraham's servant from vultures by lying over him.

By the way, this dog's appearance gave rise to the so-called shaggy-dog stories!

Spaniel: Pythagoras wrote that spaniels could store the breath of dying people as a way of keeping the spirit alive. Their tongue was said to cure skin ulcers, their presence to relieve melancholy, and carrying one would surely allay any ghostly activity around the bearer.

St. Bernard: As seen in classics such as the *Call of the Wild*, stories of St. Bernards all center around their willingness to risk life and limb to aid humans in distress.

Terrier: An interesting oddity appears in medieval tarot decks: A terrier-like dog is depicted prancing merrily at the heels of the Fool in the Major Arcana. Why this breed? Perhaps it is the aggressive energy of the terrier, its keen instincts, and its playfulness that earn it an honored designation with the Fool, who is beginning an important journey to awakening. The dog is present to guide and help the Fool with things not easily seen or sensed by humans.

Wolfhound: Some people say that St. Patrick owed his life to a dream of these animals. In the dream both he and the dogs overcame an adversary through faith. Later in Patrick's life, the story continued. Prince Dichu tried to set his wolfhound on him, but the dog would not attack. This caused the prince to reconsider his position and make Patrick an ally.

*High up in the courts of Heaven today a little
dog-angel sits and waits; with the other angels
he will not play, but he sits alone at the gates.*
NORAH MARY HOLLAND,
THE LITTLE DOG-ANGEL

THREE

DOGMA:

THE SPIRITUAL DOG

*You think dogs will not be in heaven? I tell you,
they will be there long before any of us.*
ROBERT LOUIS STEVENSON

Dogs have appeared in sacred settings around the
world, receiving attention from the gods, acting as servants of the gods, or participating in religious stories.
Some were honored as tribal spirit guides, others as
aspects of the divine, and others still were simply

welcome guests in the temples of the gods. Whatever the case, this creature has held a place of honor in many religious systems.

DOG WORSHIP

To understand animal worship, we must return momentarily to our ancient tribal ancestors whose animistic beliefs shaped their everyday lives. These people looked to nature as the most perfect representation of the divine. There were spirits in all living things, and if one could commune with, honor, and appease those spirits properly, one could also live a more fulfilling, successful life.

Since dogs were among the first domesticated animals, it is not terribly surprising that people would honor them in their religions. After all, it seemed that these creatures chose to leave the wild to accompany humankind, which set them apart in the human mind and heart. For example, among the Harranians of Syria, dogs were considered "brothers" in the occult mysteries, and as such eating this sacred creature was forbidden.

Dürer, detail from Melancholy.

Jackal-headed canopic jar.

In Mithraic tradition, the dog was venerated as a symbol of trustworthiness and sincerity. Consequently, in Persian art dogs appear regularly in the presence of Mithras, as both an ally and a friend. According to Persian myths, the great god Ormuzd decreed that killing a dog was a crime, and cherishing it a duty. As a result many important people were given the name Chan (the dog) to inspire a gentle, wise spirit. Perhaps we should follow their example!

The Japanese exhibited an odd veneration for domestic dogs as a representative of Omisto, the god of suicide. Whenever a pet dog died, it was buried standing up with its head above ground. Passersby would then leave offerings at the grave in order to appease Omisto, who can ensure the worshiper eternal joy in the afterlife.

Historical evidence suggests that dogs may have been venerated in Gaul where they were companions to Taranis, the god of lightning and death. Apparently the dogs were able to, on occasion, consume Taranis's fury and save humankind. For this service, images of dogs appear in reliefs of the Burning Wheel, which represents Taranis's fire from the sky.

Egypt is, by far, our best recorded example of an area rich in canine worship. By 3000 B.C.E. each Egyptian clan had a sacred animal that protected it. Needless to say, canines of one sort or another were favored, as exhibited in iconography from that period. In addition, the dog spirit was powerful enough to protect the dead; dogs appear in tomb art, and some were even mummified with their masters.

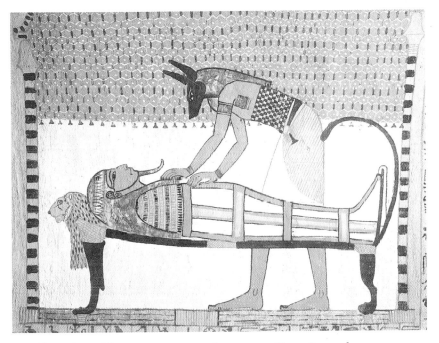

Anubis, the funerary god, seeking the heart of the deceased.

There is evidence to suggest that some Egyptians also worshiped the Dog Star, Sirius (sometimes called Sothis) as a symbol of the faithfulness one should have in the divine, and of the psychic ability one may gain through this faithfulness. This association developed rather naturally since Sirius rose dutifully at the same time the Nile's waters rose—a potent harbinger and symbol indeed. Sirius was sometimes referred to as the "sun behind the sun" and represented the cosmic secrets known only to deities such as Isis and Osiris, so worshiping the star may have been a way of honoring them.

Another excellent illustration of dog worship appears in numerous shamanic settings, including those in North America. A shaman would contact an animal spirit through trance work and mimicry, usually to attain a specific goal or to gain a particular perspective. Each creature had its own teachings and "medicine" that the shaman could draw into himself or herself. Dogs and their relatives were certainly a part of this rich tradition.

First we find the wolf spirit as an important guide, especially for groups of people. Meanwhile, coyote's spirit taunts, teases, tricks, and teaches us to laugh. Fox spirit reminds us that it's not always wise to be in the limelight, exposed. Finally, the dog spirit comes along to teach us the value of service and loyalty.

DOG SACRIFICE

Today it is hard to comprehend how and why people would sacrifice such a noble creature. In considering this practice we must understand that worshipers believed that sacred animals would have a special place with the gods they represented. In addition, offering such a valued animal would be worth more to the deity being petitioned for aid or blessings.

Generally speaking, dogs, more specifically, pups, were considered suitable offerings for the gods and goddesses of the underworld. Most often a worshiper performed a sacrifice to ask for the gift of spirit vision, something dogs supposedly possessed. By sacrificing the dog, its gift could be released to the worshiper.

Beginning in Egypt we see some ritual sacrifice of dogs as part of Anubis worship. The honored dog would be mummified afterward, often with ornamental additions so it could bear rich offerings to the god when its spirit traveled into the afterlife. Nearly all of the sacrificed dogs were young (under one year of age) and free of disease so that they would better please the gods.

Greco-Roman tradition also shows evidence of dog sacrifice, often performed in an effort to get divine relief from stifling hot summers, storms, or drought. This gives a whole new meaning to the expression "dog days," and in fact that's where the saying originates. Puppies chosen for sacrifice were most often black, which meant the sacrifice was also considered a suitable gift for Hecate if you wished safe travel or an easy childbirth.

Dogs were also killed ritually in Rome when there was a pressing sickness in the family. Romans believed that the dog could absorb the malevolent spirit associated with disease. Therefore, killing the dog would likewise "kill" the problem. This type of magical mimicry is very common throughout the world, not only with dogs but with many other animals and even plants.

The Iroquois Indians sacrificed a white dog at the start of the new year. The spirit of the dog was then to take the tribe's prayers to the next world with it. Similarly, Mayans sacrificed a spotted

Lambsprinck, De lapide philosophica.

dog during their Fire Festival, one of the most sacred observances on the Mayan calendar. When the Aztecs started facing numerous calamities, dog sacrifice appeared among a people who previously would not harm a dog because the animal represented spirits from beyond.

The Toltec Indians sacrificed brown dogs to appease the god of cacao, an excellent example of sympathetic color magic. Among the Plains Indians, a dog might be sacrificed to seal an oath, oath taking being considered the ultimate act of fidelity. The Sioux used sacrificial dogs to carry the prayers of the tribe, specifically prayers for health and longevity, to heaven.

Laplanders at least gave their deities time to decide which creature was preferred for sacrifice. Pieces of fur from several animals, including a dog, were attached to small rings hanging from the outer frame of a ritual drum. The drums were then taken to the altar. If one of the rings turned toward the image of Thor, they took it as a sign. Whatever hair was attached to that ring determined which animal became the honored sacrifice, while people sang and beat the drum.

TEMPLE DOGS

Ancient Phoenicians had a caste of priests who were fondly called dogs, but canines were not part of sacred temples in just the figurative or symbolic sense. Many were considered important companions and helpmates within a religious order. For example, in

Persia dogs roamed sacred places freely, were given "clean food," and were served before the priests and worshipers at any communal meal. As the dogs ate, people prayed. Why? Because the dog will then keep a watchful eye over the temple and alert the faithful to the presence of any malicious spirits wandering by.

It's certainly not surprising to see dogs in Egyptian temples, considering the strong canine reverence we've already discovered

Bartolomé Esteban Murillo, The Holy Family *(Museo del Prado, Madrid).*

there. One could rarely enter the temples of Hermanubis, Anubis, or Asclepius without finding a whole troop of dogs. These dogs often participated in ritual parades honoring the deities.

In Greece and Rome, dogs often guarded holy sanctuaries. Here, as in many parts of the world, the wealth of the altar tempted would-be thieves. Dogs would alert the priests to intruders or help sniff out someone who was taking home something more than a blessing. They would also warn of any evil spirit trying to encroach upon the sacred space. In addition, legends say that sacred hounds often took part in the rituals of a Sicilian war god named Adranus, likely because of their keen nose and senses.

In the Mediterranean a winning greyhound would be lavished with flowers and food, and welcomed into a sanctuary as an emblem of good luck. In Latin America the hairless dog was deified, and given all the privileges that such power and presence deserved. Swiss monks often keep St. Bernards at their monasteries, since the dog takes well to snow and cold. Temple art in Mexico shows dogs that look like Chihuahuas as a presence, and among many Native American tribes dogs were perfectly welcome at the ritual and tribal fires because they represent faith and kinship.

Moving to the Far East, the court of the Chinese emperor, which was as holy as any temple, was often filled with dogs. These were usually small, Pekingese-style pooches, who were adorned, groomed, and lavishly fed. So sacred were the Forbidden City's dogs that many people would avert their eyes if they saw one on the streets.

In Tibet, dogs such as the Lhasa apso are welcome in Buddhist temples as they were identified with both Buddha and the Dali Lama. Some of them were even trained to turn the prayer wheels of the Lamas, a service for which they became known as Prayer Dogs. In this part of the world the dog symbolizes the vigilance, insightfulness, and state of spiritual realization that humans hope to achieve.

It is interesting to note that in the Middle Ages, when the clergy wasn't as open-minded about animals in the house of god, dogs still found their way into churches and sanctuaries. The nobles, who loved their pets, insisted that the dog was as least as worthy as they to enter!

DOG NUPTIALS

While some dogs abide in temples, others get married in them. In the 1980s dog unions became a popular idea. A Universal Life minister began performing ceremonies for upward of three hundred dollars, really spectacular weddings for as much as five thousand dollars. Rumors have it that the marriage cup is laced with beef stock, and the cake is fashioned from ground lamb. One wonders if bones instead of rice are thrown at the happy couple after the ceremony!

Lest you think this idea is something totally new, in the 1930s an Indian ruler threw a lavish wedding for his favorite dog. The bride was bathed in flower water and wore a jeweled necklace, while the groom wore gold anklets. Again, in the 1960s, we read about pooch nuptials taking place in dog boutiques, complete with satin gowns, bow ties, and top hats!

In Japan, you can treat the newlyweds to a special honeymoon. The packages here generally include a reception and romantic baths. The price is similar to the wedding, about three hundred dollars—per day!

If you'd like to have a wedding for you *and* your dog, but the dating scene hasn't been cooperative, there's help available! A Maryland newsletter called *Dog Love's Junction* has ad space in the Personals for dog lovers. You might just find the perfect companion for yourself, and your pet, by reading these listings.

On a similar note, a recent study done at Indiana University involving married couples indicates that a marriage will go more smoothly and survive longer if the couple owns a dog. When dogs are present, arguments don't last as long, people are calmer, and even blood pressures are lower.

CANINE CANTICLES

In places where dogs were elevated in stature as servants or representatives of the gods, their howling or barking was often considered a kind of invocation, or at the very least an omen to

Rufino Tamayo,
Howling Dog
(Phoenix Art Museum).

which one should pay close attention. In India, for example, there are wild dogs that roam the hillsides. These creatures are called the Hounds of Heaven because of their baying, which is thought to be a prayer. It's interesting to note that today hunters still refer to the hound's bay as "giving voice."

Some of the superstitions have remained with us (see chapter 5), but for the most part dog "singing" has simply become a commercial attention-getter. The best example that comes to mind are the dogs that bark "Jingle Bells" every year; these canines even have a CD.

So strong was the human reverence toward dogs that some canine spirits continue to exist after death. The Egyptians took this concept to a pinnacle by mummifying dogs so the animals could enjoy their afterlives in a fitting form. The Egyptians left the dogs suitable food for their new existence, so they would not hunger on their path back to the gods. In part this practice had strong connections with worship of Anubis; by honoring their dogs worshipers hoped to gain more favor in the afterlife.

In Greece, the followers of the healing god Asclepius felt that their temple dogs earned a special place in the afterlife. The creatures' never-ending service in the temples was a testament to this truth. The dog's lick was regarded as having healing properties, so where better for them to live than with a healer's devoted priests?

In Mexico and surrounding regions, it was believed that dog spirits escorted each soul into the next life, and actually opened the way to heaven. We see strong evidence of this, particularly among the Mayans and Toltec. Unfortunately, this led to domesticated dogs being killed upon the death of their masters. The body was then laid next to the master's so both could reach the otherworld safely.

In Inuit tradition it's customary to keep the head of a dead dog near a child's grave. By doing so, the parents ensure a faithful

Mexican dog mask for the
tlacololero dance.

PHOTOGRAPH BY DONALD CORDRY, FROM
MEXICAN MASKS, BY DONALD CORDRY,
© 1980. BY PERMISSION OF THE
UNIVERSITY OF TEXAS PRESS.

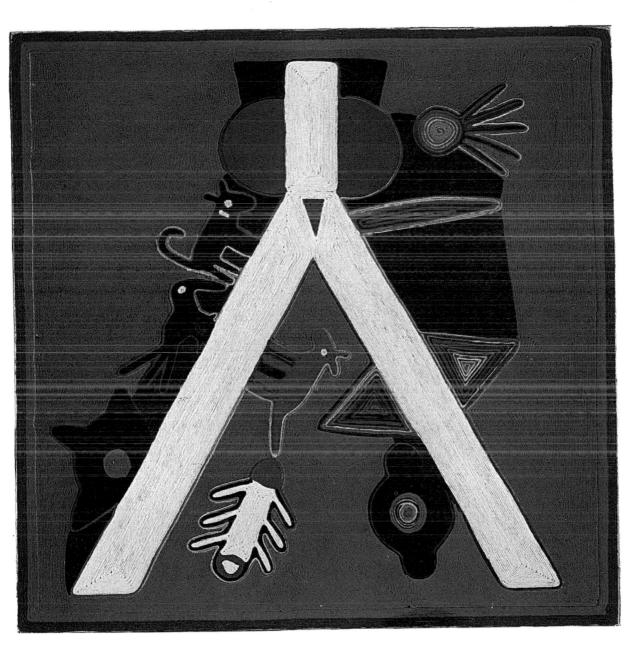

guardian who will help the young soul find its way safely into the afterlife. Ainu folklore also tells us of dogs, specifically Akitas, who live in the afterlife, in places much like their earthly homes. Other shamanic traditions say that while a dog's spirit sleeps in this world, it awakens in the Land of Shadows with other well-loved souls.

Among Christians, the belief seems to exist that if one loves his or her dog enough, that creature will be in heaven awaiting the soul's arrival. The Buddhists believe that all creatures have a soul that reincarnates—if you've ever wondered why your dog acts like a cat, the answer may lie here. Shinto tradition says all creatures have a soul, and therefore will move on from this existence into the afterlife.

Whether or not you trust in an afterlife for your dog, you can still give it a proper funeral. The ongoing love for this creature has resulted in a rebirth of pet mortuaries that last saw tremendous favor in the Victorian era. During this time it wasn't uncommon to have wakes and funerals for departed dogs complete with satin caskets, flowers, flowery obituaries, and elaborate graves. Even earlier than this, we find many historical accounts of pet cemeteries all around the world, a testament to our love of dogs.

Today we can give our departed pets elaborate care with everything from processionals to cremation. As with human funerals, this ritual seems to give pet owners a sense of closure. And, if legends hold true about the dog knowing the elemental powers and gods long before humans, we will really have little to fear when crossing death's threshold. Surely our dogs will wait for us there, and bring us to the astral realm from whence they came.

DOG MAWS AND PAWS

After dogs leave this world, some seem to be adopted by gods and goddesses, who use canines as servants or forms. Astarte can assume the form of a dog at will. Cerberus, a powerful canine spirit, guards the entryway to the Greek's underworld, barking with a voice of bronze. Greek myth also tells of a great golden dog given to Rhea, an earth goddess, as a guardian of the infant Zeus.

Here are a few examples from around the globe of canine deities, listed with thematic realms to consider in your spiritual pursuits.

Anubis (Egypt): A jackal- or dog-headed god who attends the entryway to the underworld and who is usually depicted as black. Anubis unerringly weighs the hearts of mortals to learn of their worthiness to receive rewards in the next life, even as dogs always seem to know human hearts.

Aroui (Yoruban): This god of the forest appears with a dog's head. Aroui reminds us of our link to the wild and to the animal kingdom.

Artemis (Greek): Goddess of the moon and the hunt, Artemis

Mythological scene, Piero DiCosimo (National Gallery, London).

is often depicted in the company of dogs. She is a devoted power to call upon for guidance when going through drastic changes, or when you're "hunting" specific knowledge.

Astarte (Semetic): A goddess who has a dog attribute, Astarte's name means "star" (possibly alluding to Sirius). Her domain is generally considered one of fecundity.

Baal (Phoenician): A dog-headed god who embodies ferocity and courage, Baal also brings fertilizing rain to the land.

Belit-ili (Arcadian): A dog nearby supports Belit-ili's seat of authority. She is considered a mothering figure.

Charon (Greek): Ferryman to the next life, Charon sometimes appears in the shape of a dog.

Epona (Celtic): Frequently associated with horses, this goddess of fertility and the underworld also has a canine aspect.

Gula (Sumerian): This goddess of healing is symbolized by a dog.

Opposite: Anubis and Hunefer at the weighing of Hunefer's heart.

Stone incised with the figure of a wolf (Inverness Museum).

Hecate (Greek): The patroness of witches and goddess of crossroads (representing transition and choice), Hecate is often attended by dogs.

Hunhau (Mayan): A god of death and the underworld, Hunhau is often depicted as a dog showing the soul the entryway to the next life.

Legba (West African): Legba is a trickster god who taught humans the arts of oracular interpretation and other forms of fortune-telling. His sacred animal was a dog, who also doubled as his messenger, often bringing signs.

Nehalennia (Germanic): A goddess who brings life through fertility, and who also sees the soul on its way at death, Nehalennia is shown with a dog, a ship, and fruit; she is also a patroness to sailors.

Nodens (Celtic): This god of healing has a dog aspect. This may be why a dog's lick eventually was considered to have healing virtue.

Pan-Hu (China): Pan-Hu is an ancestral dog-being to whom gifts are given during sacred observances to obtain courage, faithfulness, and protection of one's lands and family.

Quetzalcoatl (Aztec): Quetzalcoatl, often depicted as a feathered serpent, enters the land of the dead bearing the image of a dog. In Aztec mythology, Quetzalcoatl oversees practical, daily matters, always offering sound advice.

Set (Upper Egypt): This god with a greyhoundlike face has a destructive nature; however, that destruction often precedes a fresh, better beginning.

Vulcan (Greek): The god of the fire and the forge is said to have created the first dog out of bronze. Some say that when separated from his master this dog demigod became Cerberus.

Xoltl (Aztec): A dog-headed god of death and the setting sun, this god somehow became the patron of any type of ball game—perhaps because of the sun's spherical shape.

Yama (Buddhist): God and judge of the dead, Yama has a dog as one of his aspects. He is also said to have guardian qualities.

There are several ways to use the knowledge of dog gods and goddesses effectively in magic. First, you may choose to call on a canine deity when doing spells or rituals for your pets, or when calling for a familiar if you think the familiar may be dog (see chapter 4). For example, you might invoke Pan Hu to help increase the devotion between you and your dog familiar.

Second, you may look to these divine figures when you wish to develop or integrate specific doglike attributes. When you need friendship, devotion, dutifulness, courage, cunning, or spiritual insight, consider which canine best represents that characteristic, and then call on a corresponding god or goddess. You should take care and know a little of the culture in which the divine being lived, how to honor that presence in your sacred space, and how to pronounce the deity's name correctly.

Ando Hiroshige, Moonlight, Nagakubo *(British Museum).*

CANINE SPECTERS AND GHOSTS

The souls of dogs who do not find their way to the gods may continue to roam the earth as they did in life, even as the spirits of some humans do. In fact, many myths are filled with ghost dogs and dog spirits. In New Zealand, the Maoris believe that dogs have a soul that can move on to the next life. Some dogs, however, are so devoted that the spirit remains in this world until its master is ready to leave it.

In Norse tradition, Fenrir is a wolf that wanders the world chasing after the sun. At Götterdämmerung, the end of the world, he will catch it and eat it. Garm, another frightening dog spirit, announces death by howling. The association between dogs and death is mirrored in several cultures including that of Scotland where the black dog, Ce Sith, is a citizen of the fairy realm whose appearance portends death; in that of England where the Whisht Hounds hunt for souls of unbaptized children, and the ghostly Shuck represents bad times ahead; and in the culture of China where a black dog called P'eng Hen is considered to be a demon in disguise.

However, not all spirit dogs are terrible figures. There are numerous accounts of beloved pets who regularly return to their earthly residence to visit or help their masters in some way. In Lapland, for example, the household guardian spirit is often that of a departed pet dog. Dogs in this region often live lavishly pampered lives so they will serve the family well in the afterlife.

A wooden dog mask. The god Xolotl was believed to lead the dead across the river to the underworld in the guise of a dog.

PHOTOGRAPH BY DONALD CORDRY, FROM *MEXICAN MASKS*, BY DONALD CORDRY, © 1980. BY PERMISSION OF THE UNIVERSITY OF TEXAS PRESS.

Likewise, the sighting of a white ghost-dog in Wales is a positive omen; it means that a person soon to die will be guided directly to heaven.

Reports of hauntings differ in content. Sometimes only the dog's bark rings out through the darkness as a warning, omen, or greeting. Other times, the owner feels the all-too-familiar brush of the creature's fur against their skin. In still other instances, a person sees a ghostly dog image wandering its old grounds.

Such sightings have been somewhat corroborated by photographs that show dog-shaped wisps near their owners. Students of the occult are quick to point out that accounts of dog visitations are often interactive and purposeful, two things that tend to indicate a true haunting. On the other hand, there are cases in which the human notices the presence, but the dog spirit disappears or doesn't seem to heed the human at all.

The variety of personal experiences surrounding ghost dogs has led to the theory that what the person sees isn't a ghost at all, but instead a kind of memory, or an energy imprint. In the former case, the individual is so used to the sight or feel of his or her pet that certain situations evoke auditory, tactile, or visual sensations. In the latter instance, the dog's life energy so affected its earthly surroundings that a "memory" of the dog was imprinted on the area, kind of like a tape recording that can be set off by circumstances or by the presence of a sensitive person.

You may not believe that dogs have souls, or a group soul, or maybe you aren't certain what to believe, but the idea does fascinate many. What we do know for sure is that the belief in an afterlife for dogs and other creatures has enough devotees to have created a whole new paranormal industry—that of animal mediums. Just as psychics contact the spirits of dear departed humans, these mediums travel the astral realms in search of pets whose presence is sorely missed. How one can tell for sure that the right canine (or any canine, for that matter) has been reached remains an unanswered question. Perhaps the sense of peace and closure this effort gives to humans is reward enough.

For those of you who don't want to wait until your dog is gone to listen to it's wisdom, try telepathy! The Direct Book Service in Washington state offers an audiotape that teaches you how to contact your canine companion using telepathy at a far more reasonable cost than using a medium.

I agree with the dog.
REMARK MADE BY DANISH
PRINCE CONDE UPON OBSERVING
HIS PET DOG LEAVE THE ROOM
AFTER HEARING THE ADVICE OF
POLITICAL ADVISORS

FOUR
HAIR OF THE DOG

*Those that ever mind the world to win must
have a black cat, a howling dog, and a crowing hen.*
ANCIENT PROVERB

Animals of all sorts play roles in magical history. Not
all are positive, but all do imply that the symbolic powers inherent in the animal kingdom are something that
humankind has long been trying to assimilate. Canines
have been no exception to this rule.

L. LeBeau 97©

Mimbres bowl showing a hunter with two canines (private collection, used courtesy American Federation of the Arts).

From dogs being characterized as witches' familiars to the use of body parts from wolves and foxes as folk curatives, we find our four-footed friends appearing again and again in the world's mystical traditions. As you read about these practices, please remember that they evolved from animistic belief systems, in far more superstitious times than our own. Consequently, the approaches are bound to seem odd, silly, or downright gruesome to our modern minds. Nonetheless, they are part of our history, and need to be examined from that vantage point.

While we may have moved away from trusting in old wives' tales, modern magical practitioners have not lost sight of the important lessons the animal kingdom can teach us. All parts of nature represent important aspects of our spirituality to which we must reconnect. Learning how our ancestors did this, and how they used natural energy is one way to help ourselves progress along the path to enlightenment, making meaningful changes suited to our times.

DOG TOOTH

Preceding page: Lynndee LeBeau, Foxes *(Vashon Island).*

In the old grimoires, or spell collections, several magical spells called for rather unsavory uses of canine parts. Bear in mind as you read that the use of animal parts and their blood in magical procedures is a very old custom. Animals were originally used in the belief that they could provide the magician with their best attributes. Because it was the font of life, blood added power.

Beyond this, early mages often subscribed to the school of thought that says, "The worse it sounds, the better it works." Why? Because any offensive spirit would certainly not remain in a body when the cure is worse than the problem! In addition, magicians sometimes hid true magical procedures beneath the guise of odd phrases or instructions to protect their art.

Finally, remember that the old grimoires were not always a reliable source of true magical traditions because they were sometimes penned by those wishing to dethrone pagan practices through fear and misrepresentation. So between the magicians' secretiveness and the ill will of those who would put them out of business, there remains little information, other than that from oral traditions, to help modern researchers sort fact from fallacy. For example, when we read that necromancers used dog blood on linen to inscribe curses, this "blood" may actually have been an herbal preparation the components of which the wizard wanted kept secret. Or this information may have been written to inspire antipathy in an already superstitious public.

While I've limited the list below to *Canis familiaris,* the dog's relatives were not left out of such beliefs. For example, in Ireland a fox tooth was considered an excellent cure for leg swelling, fox tongue was used to encourage slivers and thorns to loosen themselves, and tongue cut from a living fox and then dried was

Nootka wooden mask used in the Wolf Dance.

a cure for cataracts. In other parts of the world, fox testicles are listed as a surefire cure for impotence and an aphrodisiac; the liver, when mixed with wine, is cited as a cure for asthma; and roasted fox lung is said to aid breathing disorders.

Hyena whiskers were used in image magic and necromancy. Its skin, when worn by a human, kept magical charms at bay, especially fascination. Carrying a hyena's tongue in your left shoe kept the people around you quiet at night, and hyena marrow applied to the skin as an ointment was thought to alleviate back pain.

Old French and Latin texts advocate using wolf skin to prevent hydrophobia, wolf flesh as a ward against ghostly visitations, and a wolf's head placed under your bed to offset insomnia and nightmares. Old English tradition says that the right eye of a wolf worn as an amulet brings victory; hair from the tip of its tail is an excellent component in love potions; the eyetooth, if worn, prevents madness; the skin, if attached to a door, keeps magic firmly outside; and the hair from a wolf's genitals, when burned, keeps people faithful!

Here are some other spells and methods from the past that include dogs or canine parts among their required ingredients, procedures, or instructions.

- To banish sickness, write in blood the name of the afflicted person on the skin of a dog. Chase the dog away and the sickness will go with it. This spell represents a typical format for disease transference.

    Alternatively, keep a dog's skin for this purpose after the creature has died and burn or bury it to banish the malady.
- A twelfth-century herbal shows dogs digging up the very magical mandrake root. This practice maintained the potency of the herb and safeguarded the mage against the spirit thought to abide there. Any human hearing the shriek of the mandrake when it was pulled from the ground would surely go mad and die. After this elaborate ritual, one should leave money on the ground near where the plant lived to double the herb's potency.
- The heart of a canine carried on the left side will keep dogs from barking at you.

- The blood of a black dog smeared on walls will break bewitchment of any kind. (This spell comes from the Apocrypha.)
- Fry the hair of a rabid dog with rosemary and eat it to cure a mad dog's bite. (This is a type of sympathetic magic, and it is how we came by the phrase "hair of the dog that bit you.") Note too that eating the hair here is a symbol of having power over the dog and its ill spirit.

  An alternative Gypsy tact was to fry the hair lightly in oil with fresh rosemary, mix this with wine, then apply it as a poultice to the wound. Oddly enough the antiseptic qualities of both the wine and rosemary may have helped!

  The Egyptians simply applied garlic mixed with another plant to the wound and spoke incantations over the poultice to speed healing.
- If you want to befriend any dog, bind the right eye of a wolf to your right side before the meeting.
- To recognize the presence of spirits and remain safe from them, eat a dish of dog or wolf meat for dinner (an Anglo-Saxon tradition).
- To cure convulsions, the folk magicians in England recommended that one consume the heart of a white hound baked in meal.
- To raise a wind that will last nine days, obtain a stone from a black dog's innards. Tie it with horse hair to a stick, and twirl the stone in the air clockwise to summon the wind. Bury the stick in the ground to cancel the spell.
- To cure fever, Saxon tradition recommends hanging from the patient's arm the right foot shank of a dead black dog because

it "shanketh the fever." A far nicer alternative comes from France, where hairless black dogs were made to lie down upon patients to absorb their sickness.

- If you wish to see invisible items or people, dab the blood of a dog on your eyelids.
- To cure jaundice, the head of a mad dog pounded and mixed with wine was the remedy of certain Scottish cunning folk. Anything of the recipe's ingredients that remained could be burned and applied to skin cancers to "cast out the foulness." Alternatively, save puppy dung, dry it, and administer it in a potion. When rose water is added to this mixture, it also cures ulcers.
- Puppy fat added to ointment inspires longevity and faster recuperation.
- The ancient Egyptian cure for eczema was a blend of canine feces and blood. If this sounds odd to you, consider that they cured baldness with a hound's leg and the hoof of an ass, removed hair with canine menstrual blood, and used a dog's tooth as an amulet to protect the bearer from rabies!
- To make yourself courageous, blend together the eye of a fierce black dog with dried snakeskin and some wine. Mix this with a feather, then drink one-third of the potion each night over the three nights of a full moon.
- The gall of a black dog made into perfume turns away witchery and evil spirits.
- To cause discord, place a stone bitten by a mad dog into someone's drink.
- Burning the eyes of a black dog was once thought to help summon spirits.

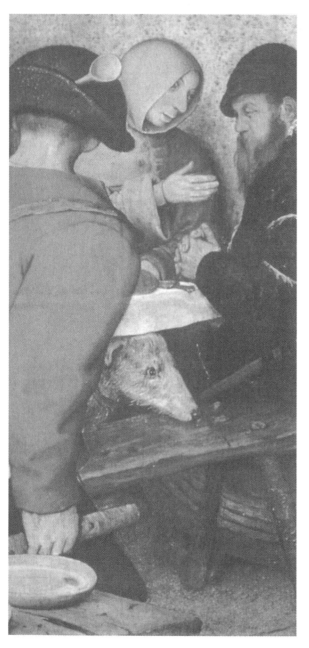

- To get a man to love you, dry the gall of a female dog and powder it. Add this to his drink and he will love you truly.
- To get rid of a cold, take one of your hairs and put it into a piece of bread. Feed this to a dog. If the dog coughs afterward, your cold will soon vanish.

We can all be thankful that for all animals such practices went by the wayside in favor of more animal-friendly, non-manipulative magical approaches. Under *no circumstances* do I suggest you try any of the aforementioned for obvious reasons, and also because these spells do not adhere to modern standards for positive spiritual living.

A FAMILIAR FACE

A familiar is defined as an animal that is associated with a witch as an attendant, servant, companion, and messenger between the worlds. Certain shamanic traditions indicate that a canine may be the familiar spirit of a magician or a shape-

Pieter Brueghel, detail from The Wedding Feast *(Kunsthistorisches Museum, Vienna).*

shifted shaman, or may house the spirit of someone who passed over. In Europe people believed that white dogs could be the familiars of fairies. In the North American shamanic tradition, dogs were rarely put to death for their magical roles. Conversely, in both Europe and America, dogs ranked high on the list of potential familiars, often succumbing to the same fate as their masters accused of witchcraft: burning, drowning, hanging, and other unpleasant ends.

Exactly how dogs gained this reputation as familiars is something lost in the pages of history, but I suspect several factors played a role. The dog's uncanny ability to sense people's true intentions is often unsettling. Additionally, superstitions about dogs having second sight, myths connecting dogs with the underworld gods and goddesses, and numerous bits of lore that talk of animals as helpmates to diviners and witches were all likely factors contributing to such beliefs.

One of the most famous of all dog familiars is the black dog owned by the wizard Cornelius Agrippa, who some people claimed was the devil in the shape of a dog. Such pets were not only associated with famous figures, however. A witch named Magdalena Crucia was often seen in the company of a dog, as was Simon Magus. Some stories claim these canines made no shadow—a sure sign of witchery and familiar relations.

In modern metaphysical traditions people still believe in familiars, but define them slightly differently. Familiars are magical partners, trusted friends, and companions—certainly not mere pets nor anything that resembles a demonic ally. These creatures have a unique rapport with their human counterparts and a deep, abiding kinship that expresses itself in both mundane and spiritual ways.

A familiar will likely respond to you attentively when you call, eagerly greet you at the door, and lounge or prance happily in any area where magical energy abides. The dog may develop unique ways of communicating its desires to you, and may even seem to sense when you need its assistance with a particularly difficult magical or mundane matter.

Dog familiars also provide their human counterparts with insight into people and situations. Frequently, the dog will shun or bark at a person carrying excess negativity, for example, or one who wishes to harm its human companion. Canine familiars protect one's home by watching activities that humans cannot see, and potentially recounting those things through dreams or gestures. For those with children who have "invisible friends," dog familiars can use their second sight to confirm the presence of spirits or fairies by playing with these friends. These services are above and beyond the familiar's aid in magical settings, such as during divination when a dog familiar might bark or howl when a significant tarot card is pulled.

How does one come by a canine familiar? It can be a difficult quest, since many times what we think we need and what the universe provides are two different things. However, there are ways to call for a familiar using items that dogs love as magical helpmates for the rite.

To begin, gather together some dog biscuits, a bowl of canned,

A witch riding a black dog to Sabbath.

Billy, king of the Macquarie, with wife and dog (Macleay Museum).

good-quality dog food, and a toy (such as a chew bone) and go to your door. Place these items just outside the door and close it. You might wish to request the assistance of a canine deity at this juncture, to better direct your energy (see chapter 2). Close your eyes and visualize your home, your face, and your neighborhood. Extend that vision outward so that a receptive animal can follow the energy to its source. A true familiar does not need, want, or deserve coercion to come to you. Keep the vision strong and focused until you somehow sense the message is being received.

At this point in the ritual, open your door to symbolically open the path for your familiar. Gather up the items left there, bringing them into the house even as you hope to bring in your familiar. Keep the tokens in a safe place (the freezer may be the best place for the canned food) until a familiar makes itself known to you, then give them to the creature (if it is, indeed, a dog). Note also that even if you're not meant to have a dog familiar, this ritual is an excellent way to find just the right pet for your home.

If a canine familiar arrives, you may wish to improve your rapport with it. Scottish witches sometimes perform a spell to accomplish just that. During this ritual a silver charm is blessed and placed on the collar of the familiar; the creature is then offered a gift of food and water. You may wish to adapt this concept, finding an appropriate gifting token, such as a name tag with your phone number on it, for your dog. Bless and energize the token and gift before making the presentation, then spend a good amount of time petting and praising your dog afterward so the energy can begin its work.

I should mention at this point that some people who perform this ritual to call for a familiar might be answered by a wolf, fox, or other member of the canine family, especially if they live in a rural area. When this happens, its obviously difficult to get too close to the animal for safety reasons. In this case, I suggest leaving small gifts for your familiar out in a wooded area during the day. As you put the items out, visualize the gifts, where they are, and yourself, and send that imagery to the creature who responded to your call. This way it can find the tokens and enjoy them before other animals do.

Note that a wild familiar will usually appear only in times of great need as a kind of omen. The animal's movements and general demeanor will help you determine what its message is. For example, if your fox friend suddenly seems very skittish and wary, maybe you should slow down and take your time when making an important decision or at the very least be sure that what you've been told is the truth.

DOG TOTEMS AND POWER ANIMALS

In shamanic traditions, people sometimes become aware of an animal guide or totemic spirit that walks with them. In some cases, this spirit represents the person's truest nature. Here the totem is a lifelong emblem that one can focus on for development and personal understanding.

In other instances, a totem may appear temporarily to highlight characteristics a person needs to develop and to help with this transition. For example, if you begin having dreams in which a dog comes to you and teaches you things, if canines begin appearing in odd places and at odd times in your life, or if a dog pops up in the media everywhere you look, you may have a canine spirit trying to get your attention. Exactly what a totem may mean is very personal. Consider the type of canine that has come to you (see chapter 1), what personal meaning that dog may have, and what's happening in your life to help you understand the significance of the totem more fully.

A painted resin sculpture from the Diyari people of the Lake Eyre district (South Australian Museum).

Here are some examples of dogs and what they may symbolize when they begin appearing regularly in your life.

Bush dog: A bush dog may warn of impending trouble if you're not observant and need to strengthen your ties to your family or community.

Coyote: The need to develop, augment, and effectively use your sense of humor and to focus your communication skills could be coyote's message.

Dingo: Spend time learning when to speak and when to remain silent.

Domestic dog: Faithfulness, protection, companionship, awareness, and diligence are all part of the domestic dog's message.

Fox: Learn how to make decisions quickly. Develop a cunning, more astute sense of things. Practice shamanic shape-shifting methods. Improve your luck.

Hyena: A hyena is a totem of magical mimicry and the power of laughter.

Jackal: Guidance, especially on otherworld journeys, is provided by the jackal.

Wolf: Develop agility, strength, and perseverance. Find your spiritual path.

You don't have to have a dog as your guiding spirit or power animal to consult one in times of need. Shamans often undertake trance journeys to meet with the spirit of a particular animal in order to gather information or insights suited to that creature. If you'd like to try this yourself, begin by determining which canine best suits the question or need. For example, if you're having difficulties when you talk to people and often take well-intended humor as an insult, you'd want to call upon the coyote spirit for help.

Next, gather a dog's bone (one that's been lovingly chewed) and boil it clean. Decorate this as you might a magical wand with crystals, feathers, bits of cloth, or whatever pleases your eye. Make sure to add a bell or something else that rattles when you move the bone in the air. As you work, keep your purpose in mind—this object is meant to call and please the desired canine's spirit.

On the night of a full moon, sit in front of any fire source (a candle or fireplace is best). Breathe deeply and evenly. Let your spirit settle into a meditative state. Visualize yourself going through a doorway that leads to a natural setting suitable for the spirit you are calling. See yourself sitting there with the bone, and then begin shaking the bone rhythmically to call the animal's spirit. Hold the bone behind you and shake it, then before you, to the left, the right, up toward the sky, and down toward the ground. This honors all the elements and the powers of earth and sky in your quest.

Finally, place the bone before you and wait patiently. Either a canine spirit will appear or nothing will happen. If the chosen spirit doesn't come, either the time isn't right or you chose the wrong animal helper for the matter at hand. If it does come, ask your question quickly and politely and then observe its reactions. Afterward, make notes in your journal of everything that happened so you can determine the significance of the spirit's actions.

APPLIED DOG MAGIC

Canines have a firm paw in magic, and many people who have dog familiars enjoy making them a regular part of their metaphysical practices. There are numerous ways of doing this, but you should take some precautions. First, if you plan to welcome your dog into the sacred space, always watch that candles, cauldrons, and cups with liquid are placed where the dog will not upset them. Second, any herbs you work with that might harm the animal should be kept well out of reach. Other dangers for dogs include snippets of thread that, if consumed, could cut and injure their digestive tract, or athames (ritual knives) that could pierce a paw.

John Tenniel, from Alice in Wonderland.

Following are samples of magic performed for or with dogs, and magic that uses dog emblems as spell or ritual components.

Canine Charms and Spells for Humans

- In Persia, giving food to a hungry dog was considered a sure-fire spell for providence and blessings. I see no reason not to follow this example, exercising some care: place the food down on the ground instead of letting the dog eat it out of your hand.
- In Egypt, making an image of a dog in clay or bronze and offering it on a sacred fire was considered one way to banish illness and invoke a god's blessing. If working magic for health, you can consider this symbolism and perhaps carry a stone or clay figurine of a dog with you for a while, then bury or burn it to destroy the energy of any sickness it collects.
- In ancient Greece a cynotherapist, or healing dog, was called upon to help alleviate the suffering of the sick, often by licking them. It's interesting to note that such ideas were still fashionable in the 1400s when women carried rubbing dogs to relieve indigestion. In both settings results were considered magic (or at the least, an effective superstition). Today we know that the presence of dogs can lift an ailing person's spirits and lower his or her blood pressure, not to mention the physical warmth and sympathetic eye they provide. If you have an ailing friend (and he's not allergic to dogs) you might want to bring your dog for a visit to help speed his recuperation, or give him a little dog statue to keep him company.
- If you happen to visit the Dartmoor Heath and hear hounds galloping and barking at night, make a wish. The hounds are

said to belong to Herne, the Celtic god of the underworld, and they will share your desire with their master.

- To encourage devotion and loyalty in a relationship, keep the image of a dog safely stored with your marriage certificate, or find wedding rings that bear a dog carving. This is an adaptation of an old Hebrew custom.
- To protect your home from spirits, place statues of dogs in the four elemental corners of the home, facing outward to guard your space. This is an Assyrian custom but it also appeared in Babylon, where ten dog statues in various colors were used.

- To keep your dog from howling or barking when you need quiet, an old spell from Madagascar recommends that you take off your left shoe and spit on the sole. This shoe should be placed with the sole facing up near a heating vent or the fireplace. Right after that, put your hand on the place where you were seated when the dog howled, and the noise will cease.

- Egyptians carried the image of a dog or a jackal with them as an amulet of protection. If you'd like to adopt this practice yourself, find a picture or carving of an alert and attentive dog. Charge and bless it, then carry it regularly (perhaps keep it in your car).

AMULETS, CHARMS, AND TALISMANS FOR DOGS

- Place elder flowers in any areas where your dog plays or sleeps regularly. According to folklore these act as a protective amulet, keeping the animal from any maladies.
- Take a small silver bell and bless it. Attach this to your dog's

collar so that each time the bell rings it sends out positive energy for your canine friend's well-being. Bells also have strong protective powers. If possible, combine the bell with a dog tag with your name and phone number on it. Make one object silver and the other gold to combine the energies of the sun and moon to work on your dog's behalf.

- Gather small branches from a dogwood tree and break them up into small pieces. Blend these with garlic powder, placing equal amounts of this mixture in four sachets: one red (fire), one yellow or white (air), one blue or purple (water), and one black or brown (earth). Sew these tightly shut. Next, using the elemental correspondences, invoke the sacred energies and bless each. Place the sachets in their corresponding compass points: fire in the south, air in the east, water in the west, and earth in the north. These will keep your home safe for the dog, who can then enjoy the energy and herbs of the sachets.

  An alternative to this is to get small statuettes, preferably granite, of dogs at attention. Dedicate these to an appropriate dog deity, and plant them in the earth around your home.

- If you wish to keep your canine from wandering off, oil or butter its paws regularly. According to Scottish tradition this acts as a talisman, keeping the creature close to home.

- To make an amulet, charm, or talisman more powerful for your dog, rub it over its fur. The static electricity positively charges the object for use and attunes the item to that specific canine.

Canine Rituals

- Among the Hittites, sacred dogs participated in rituals designed for successful hunts. In reliefs dating from 6000 B.C.E., for example, we see a woman with an alert dog as part of a prehunting party. The dog's attentiveness was a kind of sympathetic magic. We can adapt this idea by having a dog, or the image of one, with us any time we're trying to find a lost item, hunt down an old friend, or uncover missing information through magical means.

- Another Hittite ritual includes placing the figure of a dog made of wax on a person's threshold saying, "This figure is a royal dog. Just as you do not let other men into the courtyard, do not let evil things into my home." My only suggestion here would be to find an image made of a sturdier material that can remain there for protection, or if your wax image is a candle, burn it completely and bury the wax around your residence. You may also change the wording of the charge so it's more comfortable to you.

- There is no reason why you can't perform spells and rituals for your dog when it's ill. Invoke the aid and blessing of a dog god or goddess (see chapter 2). Burn purgative incense such as fennel or sage, anoint the dog with a healthful oil such as rosemary or fennel (which also deters fleas), and provide it with a ritual bowl for a tonic prepared to alleviate its condition (see chapter 5).

- To bless your dog, create a sacred space with your pet in any way suited to your path or particular magic. Hold the creature gently, and sprinkle it with rose water while invoking an appropriate god or goddess (see chapter 2). Smudge the dog with incense from a sacred fire (a smudge stick or stick of incense is best because it doesn't scare the animal). Then thank the powers, and take time to enjoy your companion.

- Ancient farmers often passed their animals through the smoke of a ritual fire to cleanse them of any sickness and protect them. An easier, modern approach is to use a smudge stick or brazier burning with appropriate symbolic herbs. Some options here include cedar and pine, which also help alleviate any nasty pet odors!

- In oceanic cultures it's often customary to hang a piece of coral from a dog's collar for protection, specifically against illness. If the coral ever breaks, however, it must be returned to the ocean and a new piece found, as the amulet's magic is broken.

The sight of a spotted dog brings
luck in exams, if one crosses one's fingers.
Wish, and it will be fulfilled.
OLD ENGLISH SUPERSTITION

FIVE

THE BOHEMIAN DOG

Every dog has his day.
MIGUEL DE CERVANTES

Folklore and superstition are filled with animals from all environments. Our ancestors revered nature as the ultimate expression of god, and as having important missives for humankind from the sacred powers if we but knew how to understand them. Additionally,

our ancestors were quite aware that animal instincts are more attuned to the earth's rhythms, and therefore reveal to us the future of those rhythms through behavior.

For one of the most beloved creatures in history, there isn't as much superstition that centers on dogs as I anticipated. Perhaps this is because after a time we came to think of dogs as members of the family and helpmates rather than as mere animals. Nonetheless, this chapter explores folk beliefs, how these beliefs influenced human discourse, and the ways in which dogs have appeared in various divinatory systems.

PROPHETIC PUPPIES: DOG OMENS, SIGNS, AND PORTENTS

Beginning with the beliefs held in common by numerous people, we find that the type of dog and where it appears has much to do with the meaning of the moment. Among Hittites, for example, a dog that comes into your home and lies on a bed presages an unexpected good turn, perhaps by way of an expensive gift. The Scottish also seem to think this is a good sign, one that will be followed by the development of a new friendship. Conversely, if a black dog enters an Arabic home it means bad luck will soon follow.

Wooden housepost, Taiwan.

The Babylonians had one of the most technically detailed systems of dog divination. People watched the many stray dogs, using the color of the animal's fur as an indicator of meaning. For example, when white dogs entered a temple it represented longevity of some kind (for a person or situation). A red-haired dog in the same setting portended a bad ending, gray dogs revealed defeat or ruin, and golden-haired dogs forewarned of impending disasters, especially to crops.

In many areas the howling of a dog was considered a bad sign for anyone hearing it, especially if that person was about to close a deal. The omen here was one of treachery or lies involved in the transaction. Technically speaking, this form of divination was called ololygmancy (the name is derived from a Latin word meaning to "howl"), and it appears in numerous cultural settings from the United States to Arabia. A howling hound was often believed to presage death or some other dire disaster, especially if the voice came at midnight, the witching hour.

Here are some other interesting bits of folklore from around the world:

- In Scotland it was customary among some to chase a dog out the door with a bit of bread to likewise chase away bad luck on New Year's Day.
- In England if your dog will not follow you it is considered a very bad sign, often one of injury.
- A dog barking at seemingly nothing indicates the presence of a ghost.

*Opposite: Dosso Dossi,
Circe and Her Lovers in a
Landscape (National
Gallery of Art, London).*

- Accidentally catching your dog's tail in the door indicates that it might be best to stay home that day.
- A dog passing between a newly married couple is regarded as a bad omen in Scotland, often symbolizing infidelity or quarrels to come. If a dog passes between an engaged couple, the marriage will never happen. To avoid either fate, simply spit on the ground after the dog passes.
- In Israel the howling of dogs near the city gates revealed that the spirit of death was entering.
- A dog barking or howling during a birth means the child will have an unhappy life. Shakespeare recounted this belief when he wrote this section of 3 Henry VI, *"The night-crow cried, boding luckless time; Dogs howl'd . . . to signify thou cam'st to bite the world."*
- In Gypsy tradition a dog digging a hole in your garden warns of a death in the home.
- Should a strange dog begin following you, people in the British Isles take this as a sign of improved luck.
- A dog eating grass and rolling on the ground is said to precede rain.
- A dog hiding under the table forewarns of thunderstorms or earthquakes. Other indicators include panting, whining, running madly around the house, and nervous itching.
- Dogs can find their way home over long distances because of their psychic connection to their masters.

IT'S A DOG'S LIFE:
DOGS IN PROVERBS AND SAYINGS

Dogs linger on the edges of and are ensconced neatly within human civilization. So it's not surprising that our language has adopted various canine references as part of popular aphorisms, proverbs, and sayings. Here are just a few with information about how and why they originated:

Mosaic from first-century Pompeii, "Beware of the dog" (Museun Nazionale, Naples).

- *Dogs always know:* This saying originated with the belief that dogs have a sense of both our supernatural and physical beings.
- *Top dog:* We call someone who is a good leader or very successful the top dog because when dogs live in packs inevitably one of them takes on a powerful leading role. To gain this position the dog must fend off would-be challengers, and also lead most defensive efforts on behalf of the pack.
- *Young whippersnapper:* While a somewhat antiquated phrase in today's society, this once applied to both young, active puppies and boys who seemed to behave similarly. It may have connections to the old rhyme that says boys are made from "snakes and snails and puppy-dog tails."
- *Hair of the dog:* The idea of having a drink to cure yourself of a hangover actually originated with a cure for mad dog bites. Sympathetic magical cures of the time recommended consuming a bit of dog hair, or putting it on the bite wound, to overpower the poison of the animal.
- *Twice bitten:* No, this has nothing to do with vampires! Actu-

ally the phrase started as a commentary on the lack of wisdom in many humans who, after being bitten once by a dog, perform the exact same action and get bitten again.

- *A regular Airedale of a fellow:* An expression that started in the 1920s to describe people with distinctive character.
- *Going for the throat:* This comes from the disposition of certain hunting and guard dogs who instinctively (or by training) aim for the throat on the intended target.
- *Hot dogs:* This all-American food came by this designation in the early 1900s when a cartoonist drew the image of a red hot as a dachshund, thus coining the name "hot dog."
- *To repent as deeply as the man who killed his own dog:* This phrase comes from an old myth about Gelert. A man came home and found his young son chewed to death. Seeing his dog, Gelert, covered in blood, and thinking the canine perpetrated the heinous act, he killed the dog, only to later discover a dead wolf lying nearby.
- *A lick and a promise:* This rather Victorian phrase, which pertains to tidying up clothing, may have started with ancient dog therapies in which the dog's lick was considered curative—in other words, it offered the "promise" of vitality.
- *Dog days:* In ancient Rome, the Dog Star rose just as the weather turned terribly hot. To try to offset this, the Romans often offered puppies to the gods in hopes of obtaining relief.
- *Hard-bitten truths:* This phrase came from various newspaper articles that related the story of how a woman's dog bit off the fingers of a thief. The criminal was eventually found; his deformity identified him.

- *Calling the dog:* This phrase seems to have originated in the southern United States when hunters began spinning wild tales about their expeditions. The person who told the most outlandish story was said to have "called the dog."
- *No bad dogs, just bad owners:* This adage has surfaced as more and more attention has been given to proper dog training and responsible ownership.
- *Dog watches:* In fact, this phrase has nothing to do with dogs. This is a two-hour duty that used to be called a "docked watch" but was abbreviated to "dog watch." The reason remains unknown.
- *A nose for the truth:* We owe this saying to the canine's ability to sniff out just about anything, thanks to its keen sense of smell.
- *You cannot recognize people by their clothes or dogs by their coats:* This saying became popular in the fifteenth century when it wasn't always easy to recognize a sick dog from a healthy one.
- *A dog's character:* This reference to fidelity and gentle nature is considered a compliment.
- *Like a terrier worrying a rat:* This is an old writer's saying that compliments this breed's persistence. It alludes to going after an idea with tenacity.
- *Barking up the wrong tree:* Originally a hunter's phrase, it indicated a dog who had picked up the wrong scent.
- *Take a bite out of crime:* A phrase with modern commercial origins, this comes direct from McGruff the crime dog.
- *Sick as a dog:* Again, this likely arose from mad dog syndrome (rabies), which was a huge problem in ancient times and caused terrible distress in afflicted animals.

- *To be between the dog and the wolf:* A translation of the French "entre chien et loup," this phrase is a metaphor for dusk, the dog symbolizing day, the wolf night. This saying has two potential origins. First, the relationship between wolves and dogs, wild and domestic, symbolizes choice and change. Second, there was a widespread belief that the dog was going out as the wolf was going home, so the two would meet at an impasse along the way.
- *He who sleeps with dogs gets up with fleas:* One of my personal favorites, the concept of keeping good company and staying with good "breeding" is illustrated here.
- *It's a dog's life:* It's interesting that this allegorical phrase is used both positively and negatively in language, probably alluding both to the good life that domestic dogs lead, and to the fact that stray dogs don't have such luxuries.
- *Fight like a dog:* Many early breeds were fierce defenders that often kept fighting even after dramatic injuries.
- *Beaten like a dog:* Sadly, before good training methods were developed, dogs were often brutally beaten in order to try and obtain obedience.
- *In the doghouse:* Once these little homes for dogs were developed,

Victor Brauner, Fascination (*private collection*).

the idea of banishing naughty humans to them was not far behind!

- *Biting the hand that feeds you:* During the Middle Ages, women in particular often hand-fed their pooches, and more than a few of them had to be treated for accidental nips.
- *Love me, love my dog:* A favorite saying from Spain that is emphatically restated by most dog lovers.

THE DOG WATCH: DOG SYMBOLISM IN DREAMS

Our dreams can tell us things that waking moments refuse to reveal. Throughout the history of dream interpretation, dogs stroll through the pages of books as omens and signs of things to come. Here are some examples:

Titian, detail from Venus of Ubrino *(Uffizi Gallery, Florence).*

- Seeing vicious dogs in dreams indicates a change of fortune, or an enemy in your close association.
- Dreaming of a dog biting you portends arguments.
- Being warmly greeted by a dog means that you will soon meet new friends.
- Sick dogs in dreams mean waning personal health or wealth, or a less than successful business venture.

- If you dream of owning a purebred dog, wealth will be yours.
- Dreaming of your own dog is a sign of luck to follow.
- Dreaming of dog shows is an omen that you will soon receive a favor.
- Strange dogs appearing in your dream reveal the presence of strangers who may want to harm you.
- A dog speaking to you in a dream means that you should listen closely to the advice of a good friend.
- Bloodhounds following you in a dream mean that temptation lurks on the horizon; following the hounds yourself, conversely, means that good luck is yours.
- Dogs chasing foxes in dreams reveal a situation or decision that will develop very quickly.
- Feeling frightened by a large dog in a dream is a sign that you will soon have to overcome some obstacle.
- Hyenas in the dreamscape represent bad risks or deception by a trusted companion.
- Growling dogs indicate that there are very unpleasant people around you, some of whom may have ulterior motives.
- Fighting dogs portend some kind of upset.
- Wolves in a dream indicate someone, often a friend, betraying a confidence; wolves howling reveal a secret alliance.
- Seeing a fight between cats and dogs in your dream means that you will settle or avert some problem in daily life.
- White dogs in dreams are omens of a good partnership, in business or in love.
- Dreaming of a dog following you is a sign that you will soon meet with success.

A second type of dream interpretation involving dogs is based on archetypes of human experience. In this case, the canine and its actions in your dream symbolize something else happening in your life, an aspect of your personality, or possibly a specific person. For example:

- If you normally dislike or fear dogs, dreaming of being frightened by a dog reflects unrecognized fears or self-doubts.
- A dog barking incessantly shows that you or someone you know is being overly pushy or is loudly expressing his or her opinion.
- A beautiful dog may represent faithfulness, devotion, friendship, and love in yourself or another person.
- Figuratively, a canine in your dreams may depict someone who is "dogging" you.
- A coyote in your dream may mean the need for some time alone to sort things out before making a decision. Without time to think, you'll easily be led astray.
- Seeing yourself showing a dog may reveal a desire in yourself for showmanship or winning, which may or may not be an ambition that helps you.
- A fox slinking into your yard in a dream indicates the presence of someone who is being similarly sly and sneaky in real life. A fox looking at you may simply reveal an ability for shrewd thinking; use it wisely.
- Seeing a dog's eyes or a dog in the moonlight can represent lunar characteristics that need to be explored, such as the intuitive, instinctual, or psychic nature.
- An injured dog in a dream often symbolizes a similarly injured relationship.

Opposite: Dorothea Tanning, Tableau Vivant *(private collection).*

- Chasing a fox in your dream indicates you may be chasing after a pipe dream or a love you cannot obtain; other foxes tend to indicate the presence of a competitor.
- Someone who dreams of small dogs is said to have a similarly "small" mind.
- Many-headed dogs in dreams suggest you're putting your attention in too many places.
- Seeing someone in the company of a wolf or jackal in your dreams represents suspicion of that person, often with regard to his or her motives.

HOWLING AT THE MOON: OTHER FORMS OF DIVINATION

Canines appear as important symbols in forms of divination other than dreams. For example, in tea-leaf reading the image of a dog symbolizes friendship. If the dog seems to be running, it portends the arrival of good news. If the dog is at the bottom of the cup, one should check to see if a friend is in need, whereas if it is upright and begging, someone will soon ask you for a favor.

The appearance of a fox in tea leaves indicates the presence of an unfaithful companion or someone who is using flattery to sway you. In tasseography (tea-leaf reading), the jackal is the mischief maker and gossip. Finally, the wolf is a sign of jealousy or self-centeredness either in yourself or in another. If the sign refers to another, take precautions against thievery.

Opposite: Gustave Courbet, detail from The Painter's Studio *(Louvre).*

In the Native American Medicine Cards, developed by Jamie Sams and David Carson (Bear & Company, 1988), receiving the Coyote card is a message that one needs to hone one's sense of humor, and learn not to take life (or oneself) so seriously. Usually the Coyote shows up just prior to unexpected changes, but there's something worth salvaging here . . . and laughter is the way to find that something. In a reversed position, this card warns of illusion or deceit, either from someone else or from yourself.

The Dog card represents service to others, but it is not without limits. Proving loyalty doesn't mean giving up our beliefs or crossing personal boundaries. Reversed, the Dog nips at our heels to try and keep us away from negative people or situations.

The Wolf card is one that indicates a call to teach in some form, or that a new psychic awareness is developing for the querent. When it appears reversed, it's a warning to look further and to delve deeply for understanding. Something here is hidden, outmoded, or being limited in some manner.

Finally, the Fox card reminds us that we need not always be the center of attention. In fact, sometimes remaining in the background is in our own best interest. Reversed, the Fox says you're being observed, or that you have somehow given in to negative self-images.

The tarot is another card-based divination system in which dogs appear. In the Major Arcana, which houses the main archetypes of our spiritual and physical journey in this world, a dog often appears on three separate cards. The first of these is the Fool—a small dog leaps toward the Fool who stands at the edge of a cliff.

There could be several reasons for this imagery, the first of which comes from the fool himself. The Fool is a trickster who is filled with both potential and challenge. Since the dog's relatives were also connected with tricksters, artists may have felt this companionship was natural. Alternatively, perhaps the dog is a necessary companion and helpmate to the Fool's journey, or perhaps the dog is trying to warn him about impending danger. In either case, this imagery has become accepted as "traditional."

The next card on which a dog frequently appears is the Moon. The artwork on this card shows two dogs howling at the moon, as dogs are wont to do. The symbolism here is focused on the lunar sphere as a symbol of the intuitive self. The dogs baying at this light represent our own need to recognize and work with this aspect of self. The fact that there are two dogs shows that our nature is dualistic (for example, logical as well as instinctive).

Finally, in some decks the Death card has dogs exactly where they have appeared again and again in the world's mythology: standing guard before the gate to the next world. This card seems fearful to the uninformed, but the symbolism is actually more positive than negative. Yes, something is ending but not without something else beginning. The Death card denotes the start of a new life as a psychic and spiritual being—and the dog spirit stands ready to guide us on that journey.

The Moon card from the Besançon Tarot.

Chinese astrology features the dog as a specific personality type. If you were born in the year 1946, 1958, 1970, 1982, or 1994 (a twelve-year cycle) or between the hours of 7 P.M. and 9 P.M. you come under this astrological sign. It is said those born during the year or hour of the dog will exhibit defensive alertness and tend to be loners who think long and hard about everything.

Dog people never rush and will not be rushed. They need to take care to get distance and perspective on situations before biting into them. Additionally, dog people seem to be very mindful of justice and willingly speak out where inequity exists.

In relationships dogs are, as one might expect, extremely loyal, straightforward, and honest, sometimes to a fault. A person born in the year of the dog will rarely let his mate down or disclose a confidence. Though not a great communicator and a bit of a worrywart who also cares little for money, the dog's actions still inspire confidence and trust in the people around him or her. Socrates was supposedly a dog person, as were Lenin and Brigitte Bardot.

THE DOG STAR: ASTROLOGY FOR DOGS

According to some, the ancient Egyptians so revered their dogs that they even explored how the art of astrology could be applied to them, assigning different gemstones and canine personality characteristics to different birth times. The truly dedicated New Age dog owner might want to try this system to better understand his or her companion.

If you know when your dog was born, look to the following list for more insight into its behavior and for its lucky birthstone. Consider using this stone as part of an amulet or bonding gift for your dog by placing it in the creature's collar, bedding, or in another safe decorative item placed near where the dog often plays and sleeps (see chapter 3).

January 23–February 22: This dog is variable, having the attention span of a three-year-old child. It is akin to a young soul who wants to see and do everything at once. This dog's stone is tourmaline.

February 23–March 22: This is not the best dog to choose as a family pet because it bonds to one person and avoids everyone else. Its stone is malachite.

March 23–April 22: Bouncy and vital, this dog wants your whole attention whenever possible, so make sure you have plenty of time for it. This dog's stone is jet.

April 23–May 22: This is an overly affectionate dog who licks and wants to be fondled by everyone. Avoid wearing bright colors around this creature—this will cause joyful romping and jumping. This dog's amulet stone is lapis lazuli.

May 23–June 22: A whimsical creature, this dog can be somewhat fickle and independent to the point of frustration, almost like a cat. The best charm for this canine is coral.

June 23–July 22: The epitome of a devoted best friend, this is the ultimate pet dog who wants nothing more than a home and a family. The talismanic stone for this dog is moonstone.

July 23–August 22: This dog tends to mark its territory ritually and doesn't like other pets around being the king or queen of its castle. A diamond-shaped stone (or a rhinestone) is a suitable amulet for this dog.

August 23–September 22: If you don't like messes, this is the dog for you! It will be meticulous about its appearance and enjoy grooming. Give this dog a rose-quartz charm.

September 23–October 22: A one-person canine, once you bring this dog home expect to make it a central part of everything you do. Blue topaz is a fitting amulet for this pooch.

October 23–November 22: This is a perfect dog for a familiar or totem animal because it has keen psychic awareness and insight. Give this dog a black onyx as a talisman.

November 23–December 22: Take this curious dog around your neighborhood regularly since it will want to explore at the slightest provocation and will need to scope out the territory so it can find its way home. Give it a jade charm.

December 23–January 22: This is a dog that doesn't like change, and will find moving or new family members very upsetting. Effectively, this is an old soul very set in its ways. Agate is the best amulet for dogs born during this time.

Everyone needs a spiritual guide, a minister, rabbi,
counselor, wise friend, or therapist.
My own wise friend is a dog.
GARY A. KOWALSKI,
THE SOUL OF ANIMALS

SIX

GONE TO THE DOGS

Who [god] gave the dog to be companion of our
pleasures and our toils, hath invested him
with a nature noble and incapable of deceit.
SIR WALTER SCOTT

Many dog owners say that it was not they who chose their dog, but vice versa. Some dogs wander into our lives, while others inspire our love from behind a display window. In any case, unlike a cat, who comes home to rule the roost, the dog comes home to share it.

If you are considering getting a pet dog, here are

some guidelines to follow to ensure a successful match. First, always go to a clean, well-kept pet store or breeder who has been recommended to you by a reliable source. For example, in our area we have a pet supply store that has a computerized list of places to contact for various breeds. While you can find puppies in the newspaper, there are rarely any guarantees of good health or quality of breeding. Another excellent source of both mixed-breed and purebred dogs is your local animal shelter. Animals placed for adoption have been screened for good health and have had an initial veterinary visit. Many shelters, in the interest of making their animals as "adoptable" as possible, invest time in teaching dogs appropriate behaviors and social skills. Because shelter personnel have a vested interest in finding permanent homes for their animals, they are experienced in matching people with the right pets and are happy to share their knowledge with anyone who is ready to become a dog owner.

Second, think about whether you want a young dog or an adult, and what sex, size, and type of dog you prefer. An adult may have habits you don't like, but it will probably be house-trained. A puppy is very energetic and demands both time and attention. Males tend toward more dominant behavior than females, while females usually want more attention than males.

Size is a consideration for people without yards or with small homes. A large dog needs a place to run, but small dogs also need regular exercise to stay healthy. Bear in mind where you'll have to walk your dog, and how much space you have so the animal will be comfortable in your home (and you'll be comfortable with the fully grown animal). The size of a dog does not determine its personality. About the only thing that size does seem to influence is appetite— larger dogs are generally less finicky about food and eat more of it.

As to the type of dog, consider how much time you have, if anyone in your home has allergies, and a bit about the kind of behavior you're hoping for (a guard dog, a hunting dog, a family pet, and so forth). Shedding dogs (or dander from them) can sometimes set off allergies. Long-haired dogs require more care. Purebreds can be expensive, but you can usually depend on the kind of behaviors to expect from them. Whatever your choice or options, you may want to consult a local veterinarian for more insight and interview various pet shops, animal shelter employees, or breeders before actually seeking a puppy.

Third, don't make a quick choice. Look at the puppies carefully. Watch for bright eyes, a good-looking coat, playfulness, and a healthy interest in you. A puppy with a round belly is cute, but a round abdomen could indicate the presence of worms. Check the pup's gums; if they're healthy and pink it's a good sign. Beyond this, observe the dog's personality. Does it immediately come to strangers? This type of canine makes a good pet, but not a good watchdog. Will it let you rub its belly? This is a sign of a more submissive nature, indicating a dog that won't bully other household pets, and will usually respond well to children.

Before bringing a new dog into the house make sure that hazardous substances aren't within paw's reach, even as you might child-proof a house. Here is a list of dangerous plants and other items that just aren't good for your dog:

Aloe plant: causes diarrhea
Chicken and turkey bones: source of gagging
Chocolate: too much can seriously harm your dog
Crocus: causes nervousness and vomiting
Daffodil: causes heart irregularity and vomiting
Food coloring: while a pretty red dog food might appeal to you, the added coloring may be harmful to your dog
Holly: causes vomiting and diarrhea
Lily: causes kidney failure
Poinsettia: an overall irritant to the dog's system
Rhubarb leaves: highly toxic to dogs
Salt: toxic in quantities over 2 grams per pound of the dog's weight
Vegetables (some): mushrooms and squash in particular may cause digestive troubles; onions can cause anemia

If you do have an accident with any potentially poisonous product call the poison control center of the American Society for the Prevention of Cruelty to Animals at 800-548-2423. There

Francisco Goya,
Marquesa de
Pontejos (*National
Gallery of Art,
Washington D.C.*).

is a fee for services rendered. If at all possible, try to find out what the dog consumed. It could save the creature's life.

Note that the first six weeks of a dog's life are the most important with regard to its behavior toward humans. The second six weeks are vital to overall training, in that the dog is very impressionable at that age. A puppy that has full exposure to a home and people during the first twelve weeks will make a better pet than one kept in a store or pen.

PAPER TRAINING

It is not difficult to train a dog, but it is harder than housebreaking a cat. Many breeders today highly recommend crate training. For the first few months that the dog is at home, the only time they are out of the crate is to play, eat, and go outdoors. A dog will not soil the place where they sleep unless desperate and so will whine to go out.

For those of you who think this sounds like a terrible fate for your puppies, let me reassure you. My dog, Mozart, loves his "room." This is his personal space, akin to a den, where he often retreats of his own accord to be alone. When I correct Mozart, he's told to go to his room just like a child, and he does. I do not lock him in as punishment, however, anymore than I would my son. He can travel in this crate if need be, so he's more comfortable on the road.

The crate trains both the owner and dog to get the timing

right. The only caution is that puppies will cry at night for a while, and it's hard not to give in and let them out. If you do this, however, you'll have to go back to regular paper training, which is not as quick or as successful as the crate.

For those without yards, most dogs love to be walked, but leash training can take a little time. Remember that puppies especially want to romp and play rather than pay attention to the business at hand. Begin by using a six-foot lead and practice indoors with your dog so it gets used to the feel of both the collar and leash. If your dog is large, you may want to consider a halter over a collar as it will provide you with greater control.

On those occasions when the dog has an accident in the house, a warm solution of 3 parts vinegar to 1 part water or a mixture of 2 parts water and 1 part each of borax and ash will help in cleaning. Items that can't be washed need to be sprayed with a commercial enzyme (available at pet shops) to really get rid of the scent, otherwise the dog might return to that spot again and again. If you can't get an enzyme spray immediately, try sprinkling a little pepper on the spot—it will make the dog sneeze and therefore be less tempting.

Teaching dogs to stay off furniture is sometimes difficult. They, like humans, enjoy comfort; dogs also like being close to anything that

smells like their owners. As for cats, having a squirt gun might help deter this behavior without too much scolding. Citronella essential oil may help—mix a few drops of oil with your furniture polish or wash water. Dogs don't seem to like this scent, and it's perfectly safe to use.

Another ongoing struggle for indoor dogs, especially puppies, is chewing. Like human babies, puppies are teething and chewing is a necessity. Unfortunately, what the dog chooses to chew isn't always what you might wish. Have several solidly made chew toys ready. If you find your puppy with an item you don't want chewed, take it away with a stern reprimand, then offer the toy alternative. Over time, your dog will get the idea.

Other helpful hints for solving your dog's bad habits include:

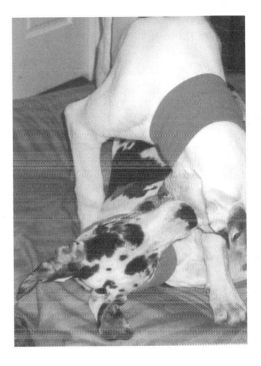

- **Face licking:** Blow at the dogs face and firmly say "no."
- **Leg mounting:** Try lifting your knee firmly into the dog's chest.
- **Feces eating:** Sprinkle hot sauce on the remains and try adding pineapple to your dog's diet. The fruit has enzymes that your dog may be lacking.

If nothing else seems to work, you can resort to professional training or perhaps consider crystal therapy. A rose quartz helps difficult dogs break bad habits, and amber absorbs excess energy from overly active dogs.

Opposite: Auguste Renoir, The Boating Party Lunch (Phillips Collection, Washington, D.C.).

CANINE BODY LANGUAGE

Okio, Puppies
(The Kokka).

Dogs have ways of making their emotions and desires known just as humans do, but our understanding of these messages is often lacking. For example, many people interpret a dog's bark as prelude to an attack. This isn't the case at all. Usually a dog barks by way of alerting his or her owner, or other dogs, to a specific presence or happening. Attacks, on the other hand, are preceded with silence or snarling.

A howling dog is one that is trying to find other dogs. This behavior comes from the days of traveling in packs, when howling enabled the dog to find its companions over distances when the group became separated. A human who joins in his or her dog's song will be warmly received.

Tail wagging is among the most difficult behaviors to interpret correctly. A dog that wags its tail in short bursts combined with raised hairs or snarling isn't happy. A dog that wags widely with little control is more friendly and submissive to humans, while one that holds its tail low is very submissive. Wagging as dogs greet each other can be a sign of uncertainty, welcome, or even a come-hither pass. The best way to discover which is which with your own dog is to observe and take mental notes.

Most people recognize that a dog with its tail between its legs is frightened. The dog does this to try and hide the scent glands that abide in that area, and therefore "hide" themselves from reprimand or other threats. In some cases, however, a dog may let its tail droop simply to show it is not a threat in a particular situation.

Following are other behaviors that we might misinterpret or simply not comprehend.

- Jumping up and licking faces is not a sign of aggression, but actually a sign of submission. This is how puppies ask for food or grooming from their mother.
- A dog may lay on its back as another submissive move or it may be asking for affectionate belly-rubbing.
- A bowing dog (one with its back end up, front end lowered, and head looking up) is asking you to come play. One that appears to smile without showing any teeth, paws at its owner, prances friskily, or puts a toy between its owner's feet is also asking to play.
- Nervousness can be caused by strange people, unique noises, odd environmental changes, and separation from its human owner.
- Wide-eyed looks are usually an invitation to play, but might signal a fight if other body language is aggressive. If the dog's head is at a comfortable angle

Gallo-Roman dog found at the Temple of Nodens, Lydney, Gloucestershire.

and it is not growling or snarling, the dog is showing a passive, "play with me" look.

- Fear of loud noises or a startle reflex is quite normal, but can be disturbing for human owners as they watch their dog cringe through a thunderstorm or fireworks. Try putting a few drops of mineral oil in the dog's ear. The oil acts as a buffer and will lessen the creature's sensitivity to sound.

BONES TO GO

The feeding of a dog can prove confusing to humans. Dogs love fresh meat, but have omnivorous tendencies. Some of

The Greedy Dog and His Bone *from the* Kalila Wa Dimna.

our table foods are okay for dogs, but you shouldn't give them too much in the way of table scraps unless you are familiar with dietary guidelines for your animal. For example, both white and brown rice are great foods for dogs with stomach problems just as they are for humans. Chicken is also good for dogs because it is easily digested, but requires some rice or bread to balance out the meal.

Canned foods vary dramatically in quality and content. It's generally recommended that you buy a premium dog food, such as those stocked at pet supply stores, for greatest nutritional value. Also, this should be mixed regularly with dry food to help keep the dog's teeth and gums healthy. Semimoist food is very high in calories, so it is not recommended for overweight dogs. Note too that many pet food manufacturers are starting to make specialty blends for dogs with special needs, such as low-calorie food and tartar-control food. Ask your veterinarian to recommend a couple of brands suited to your dog's unique needs, weight, and activity level.

If you have more than one dog in the house, give them each their own dish and provide plenty of fresh water each day. Some dogs become very possessive of their dog dish (kind of like humans and coffee cups); having separate ones alleviates territorial fights.

ON THE ROAD

Traveling with any animal can be tricky and risky. There are many types of dog carriers available, one of which will fit your car, budget, and your dog's size. For cars, crate-trained dogs will take well to having their crate in the car if it will fit. If the dog has to be free, try teaching it to adjust to

a safety belt. Also, if you're traveling over long distances, remember to stop and let the dog walk, stretch, and drink water. *Never* leave a dog unattended in a car because it could get overheated.

If traveling by air, call the airline ahead of time and get details. Some require veterinary papers (shot history and health records), and these are good to carry with you anyway in case of emergency. Mark you dog's cage clearly with the words LIVE ANIMAL, and make sure the dog has proper identification on its collar. Some small dogs may accompany you in the passenger compartment with the proper carrier and the airline's permission. If your dog is particularly skittish, however, consult your veterinarian about possible tranquilizers.

If you have to send the dog into cargo, make sure the crew knows the creature is there. Paperwork can get lost. Make sure your dog's crate is marked inside and out with your home address and destination, and that your dog has a suitable identification collar. Finally, double-check that your crate has the correct destination tag, put a water dispenser in the crate, and avoid taking your pet when it is very hot or cold as weather drastically effects temperatures in the cargo hold.

Think ahead, and check with your reservations clerk to make sure the hotel allows animals, and under what circumstances. Travel agencies can often tell you what lodges and hotels are pet friendly.

Other smart ideas include the following:

• Bring a recent picture of your pet in case it should get loose.

- Maintain your pet's feeding schedule as closely as possible to help it adjust to any time changes and the overall stress of travel.
- Pack a few of the dog's toys so it has familiar objects to make it feel at home. Include a piece of your old clothing as a "rug."
- Freeze some water in a dish so it melts slowly along the way.
- Bring extra leads. These inevitably get lost in odd spots and you'll need a backup.

HOME AGAIN, HOME AGAIN

When a dog strays it causes its human owners much worry. However, it is helpful to know that numerous experiments and true-life stories reveal that dogs have a remarkable homing instinct. While scientists don't fully understand how it works, dogs seem to have an internal compass of sorts. So, look

Anonymous, The Spinet Concert
(*National Museum, Nuremburg*).

around for your canine, shake its food bag, and leave out food and drink. Unless something is terribly wrong, or the dog gets taken in by a good Samaritan, it should find its way home.

There are certainly extra steps you can take to ensure that your dog stays safely at home, or if your pet does stray, that it will be returned. First, make sure your fence or dog run is secure. Some dogs are very good at squeezing out of small openings between the fence and ground, or strong enough to pull out a lead that's only loosely planted in the earth. When walking your dog, make sure its collar is tight enough so it doesn't slip off with a good tug, but not so tight that it chokes the animal.

Second, acquaint your dog with your neighborhood's sights and sounds. Take it on regular walks over several different routes. In time, the dog will begin to recognize sights and smells on these routes, which will help it find home should it ever get loose. Additionally, the dog is less likely to be startled by the noise of automobiles, lawn mowers, and so forth. These noises, if unfamiliar, can cause a dog to run much faster and farther than it might otherwise.

Third, keep some of the dog's old toys and a piece of your old, unwashed clothing stored somewhere. Putting these in various locations outside the house may add just enough scent to the air to help a dog nose its way home.

If, in the end, you have to advertise your pet's disappearance, make sure you leave out some distinguishing details so you can confirm the "right" find. Also make sure to contact local kennels and the ASPCA with this information. If someone calls claiming to have your dog, do not send money. Go in person to retrieve your pet to avoid being scammed.

PET CARE

Living in a rural area and diligently keeping up with your dog's immunizations are the two best things you can do for your pet; the former may not be under your control, but the latter certainly is. Other helpful things include learning a little first aid and being aware of your dog's changing physical needs as it gets older. At least once a month, spot-check your pet for fleas, sore spots, redness, odd discharge, and aromas that don't seem normal. You can turn this into a game, and give treats while you look at all areas, such as between the toes, in the mouth, ears, eyes, and so forth. By doing this regularly you could uncover a threatening problem before it gets out of control.

At least once a year after the initial immunizations, take your dog for a complete exam by a good veterinarian. Talk to dog owners in your

Greek statue.

neighborhood or with family members to see who they recommend. The veterinarian can help you with problems that are hard to lick at home, such as any allergies the dog may develop.

Take the time to pet-proof both your home and yard. If you keep toxic substances in your garage, make sure they're up above the dog's reach, for example, or don't let the dog near that area. Likewise, I put my dog outside while I'm cleaning so he's not exposed or trying to play with cleaning supplies that can be very harmful.

Another big risk to dogs in many homes is unsecured electrical cord. The animal might chew these, or trip over them and bring down a heavy object on its body. This can be pretty easily remedied by getting a package of cable guards that allow you to secure wires and cords to the wall or floor, leaving nothing loose or tempting.

Besides those already listed, beware of these common household items that pose a threat to your dog if consumed:

Antifreeze fluid	Medications
Brake fluid	Paint chips
Coins	Pins
Diapers	Plant food
Foil	Polish
Garbage	Twine

Take care of your dog's coat, eyes, and teeth regularly. Brush and bathe the dog from the time it's young. The mitts that cover your hands seem to work very well; the dog feels like it's being petted. As you brush, remove any globs of dried matter from near the dog's eyes, get rid of tangles, watch for fleas or ticks (and remove them), and then finish by brushing your dog's teeth and gums. There are special canine toothpastes available, and even older dogs can learn to adjust to cleanings if you start slowly. Most veterinarians offer this service, too.

Several natural and herbal remedies seem to work effectively with dogs. By far the most popular these days are natural flea deterrents such as lavender, fennel, cedar, mint, sassafras, rue, and eucalyptus. These herbs can be powdered, made into tinctures for applying to the dog's fur, packed into a sachet near its bed, or used when washing the floors. Also, according to experts, the scent of lavender, jasmine, sandalwood, and chamomile are excellent at keeping a dog calm.

For another New Age approach, try color therapy. Color therapy is based on the idea that color has vibration, so don't worry that your dog won't be able to see the color as

Paolo Uccello, detail from The Hunt in the Forest *(Ashmolean Museum, Oxford).*

well as you do—it will be able to sense it nonetheless. Follow this basic guideline, adding the suggested color to your dog's environment wherever possible:

Yellow: energizes a solemn or sluggish dog
Blue: calms an overly playful puppy
Green: instills confidence in a fearful dog
Red: encourages copulation
Gray: instills independence in your dog (especially if you're gone for long periods)
Brown: keeps a dog from wanting to run off so much
Black: increases your dog's overall energy and attention span (best used in small amounts—too much can become depressing)
Purple: increases your dog's fun-loving nature or appetite

Here are some helps and hints for dog first aid and health care that you can do at home:

BLEEDING

Apply pressure to the wound with your hand. If this doesn't work and the injury is on a limb, tie a small piece of cloth above the area and get the dog immediately to a veterinarian.

BREATHING

Mouth-to-mouth resuscitation works on dogs as well as humans.

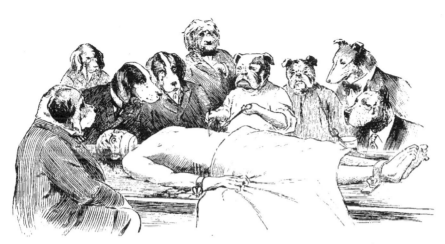

Just take care not to breath too hard. Remember that dogs have much a smaller lung capacity than do humans.

Broken Bones

Wrap the animal in a blanket or towel to keep it from moving, then transport it to a care facility.

Burn

Apply a mixture of 1 part cider vinegar and 1 part cool water. Afterward bathe the area in aloe gel, yogurt, or honey.

Choking

Look inside the dog's mouth to see what is causing the problem. Use one hand to keep the dog's mouth open and the other to retrieve the object. If this doesn't work, try holding the dog up by the back legs and gently swing. As a last resort, you can try the Heimlich maneuver—a thrust to the diaphragm—but be careful. This can cause damage if done too hard, including broken bones.

FLEAS

Add a bit of brewer's yeast and garlic powder to your dog's diet two to three times a week. Always begin flea prevention two to three weeks before the start of the season, and continue it for two to three weeks afterward to keep fleas out of the house during winter.

Electric flea collars often don't work effectively. They aren't recommended, but if you try any brand make sure you get a written guarantee that provides enough testing time to substantiate the cost.

GAS

Feed your dog smaller meals throughout the day rather than one large meal. Charcoal pills are also said to help alleviate this problem.

HAIR BALLS

Give your dog a little vegetable oil or lard. Let them lick it off your hand so that no other foreign substances are introduced.

HEAT

If an animal shows signs of overexposure to the heat, wash it with a cool cloth (not cold) and slowly give it water. Do not let it lap up too much or it will become ill.

ITCHING

If your dog likes baths, try old-fashioned oatmeal soap to combat the scratching. Otherwise, dab a little warm oatmeal on the affected areas.

JOINT SORENESS

Rub a rosemary tincture on the affected area. A few drops of tea tree oil diluted in olive oil also seem to help.

MITES

A drop or two of warm, garlic-laden olive oil drowns the mites and also eases itching. (Strain any garlic bits from the oil before applying.) You could also clean out the dog's ears with a cotton ball soaked in a little wormwood oil.

POISON

If your dog has consumed something it shouldn't, give it milk blended with egg to absorb the toxin until help can be reached. If possible, bring along a sample of what it has consumed.

SHAMPOO (DRY)

Use equal amounts of orris root powder and cornstarch to which

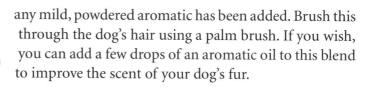

any mild, powdered aromatic has been added. Brush this through the dog's hair using a palm brush. If you wish, you can add a few drops of an aromatic oil to this blend to improve the scent of your dog's fur.

SKIN IRRITATION

To 1 cup of oil or vinegar add 10 drops of thyme or mint essential oil and dab it onto the sore regions. You may want to first test this solution on a small area of your dog's skin.

TICKS

Loosen the tick from the dog's skin using vinegar, alcohol, or an oil soak, then remove it with tweezers.

WORMS

Feed your pet garlic and sprinkle a thyme tincture on its food.

By the way, you can now purchase medical insurance for your dog. There are several pet insurance groups in approximately forty states. Ask your veterinarian which group, if any, they honor and what benefits the insurance offers.

THE TRIVIAL DOG

Dog books and magazines are filled with odd facts and bits of information about man's best friend. Trivia is tremendously fun to share with other dog lovers at home, on airplanes, and anywhere you may end up conversing about your beloved pooch.

- A dog's lick isn't really harmful to people. In fact, your dog can probably catch more from you than you can from it!
- Some people reprimand dog owners about overly pampering their pets. Nonetheless, recent studies indicate that babied dogs have fewer behavior problems.
- Speaking of behavior, so many dogs in human history have proven themselves heroic that Ken-L Ration Dog Food Company honors dog heroes every year. The dog considered most deserving gets a whole year's supply of dog food!
- California has the highest population of dogs in the United States, numbering nearly six million.
- Physically challenged dogs have almost as many options available to them as their human counterparts (except perhaps for support groups). For example, we owned a dog that broke her back and absolutely loved the dog cart that allowed her to run and romp with the other dogs.
- If you're ever in a situation where your dog is stolen and someone requests that you come pick up the pooch in a special location, beware. This is a new method being used by burglars to lure people away long enough for them to empty the house.
- While many people go to a shelter thinking to get a mixed-breed dog, over 25 percent of shelter dogs are purebreds.
- If your pooch is particularly talented or does really odd things, send a videotape to David Letterman's animal coordinator, Ms. Sheehan, at The Late Show, 1697 Broadway, New York, New York 10019.

- Dogs who succeed in show business can get sunglasses so they won't be recognized. These are available in the same stores that sell sunscreen for the Bahama-bound dog, and lighted leashes for pooches who love the night life!
- Just when you thought you'd heard it all: did you know there are indoor toilets, outdoor videos, in-house manicurists, and even in-place treadmills for our beloved dogs?
- The ultimate gourmet treat for your dog is dried liver. Trainers often use this.
- The canine sense of smell is over forty times better that of the average human. This is likely a way of compensating for the dog's vision, which doesn't recognize details well and only sees in black, white, and pastels.
- If your dog seems to have an allergy, have you checked yourself lately? Dogs can be allergic to your perfume, cologne, shampoo, and even dandruff.
- If you and your mate are getting divorced, your dog can receive support payments and even visitation rights similar to children.
- The first year of owning a dog can be quite expensive, averaging over one thousand dollars for purchase, shots, supplies, and so forth.
- Dogs can recognize the sound of your footsteps up to fifty yards away, even in a noisy area.
- Some of the most popular dog breeds are Labrador retrievers, shepherds, spaniels, beagles, and Pomeranians.
- Of the breeds, the best among large and small dogs respectively for all-around guard duty are German shepherds and terriers.
- Small dogs tend to live longer than large dogs. Large dogs reach

old age at around eight years, while smaller breeds reach "maturity" at around eleven.

- The greatest majority of dogs owned in the United States are between six and ten years of age.
- You can make a sweater from your dog's fur! That's right—long-haired breeds such as Samoyeds, keeshounds, and Newfoundlands have fur that spins well into wool-like fibers for anything that you would normally make from yarn. Neat way to recycle, eh?
- Even dogs haven't been immune to political correctness. Mutts are now fondly referred to as "random breeds."

DOG.COM

For those readers with access to the Internet and who want to learn more about dogs, there are several Web pages dedicated to our four-footed friends. Try any of the following:

- www.akc.org is the official site of the American Kennel Club (AKC).

- www.iams.com offers free trial sizes of various foods, coupons, and information on products.
- www.drsfostersmith.com provides excellent health care information and well-priced pet supplies that can be ordered through the mail or on-line.
- www.purina.com/dogs provides an alphabetical listing of breeds.
- members.aol.com/ShibaRuled/Petshop.html lists the pros and cons of finding a reputable breeder versus going to pet shops. America On-Line also has excellent pet chat rooms, but you must be a registered user.
- www.apapets.com is the site for the American Pet Association, offering information on veterinarians, pet care, and humane agencies along with an "Ask the Vet" service and more.
- www.webring.org/ringworld/misc/pets.html provides links to all kinds of information on breeds.
- www.tiggr.com/dogmall leads to the Virtual Canine Mall with links to sites selling all kinds of dog products.
- www.h4ha.org is the site for Hugs for Homeless Animals, providing a worldwide animal shelter directory, listing of lost and found pets, a bookstore, and more.

GLOSSARY

*I wonder how different life would be for me if I could be as
lacking in self doubt and self judgment as Putnam [my
dog] . . . to act as if one had the total endorsement of the
universe behind one's particular existence would be
extraordinary.*

> GUNILLA NORRIS,
> *JOURNEYING IN PLACE*

In your interactions with dog owners and breeders,
and when reading dog-related books, you may come
across some unfamiliar terms. Some of these are covered here for your reference. Please note, however,
that there exist more breeds and bits of jargon than

can be described here. For more information, contact your local pet store (as many now offer computerized pet searches), dog associations, any of the books listed in the bibliography, or surf the Internet.

Acquired behavior: While dogs are born with certain instincts, many things are taught by the pup's mother, especially certain pack traits.

Baiting: Earlier in Roman times dogs, usually mastiffs, were used to bait bulls and other animals or people.

Bandogges: An Old English term that's applied to large, selectively bred fighting dogs.

Bat ear: An ear that stands erect, being broad at the bottom and curved at the top.

Beagle Brigade: A division of the U.S. Department of Agriculture that uses dogs to find illegal food items entering the United States.

Breed: Any of a variety of domestic animals that has been cultivated with specific, identifiable characteristics (both physical and behavioral).

Breed standards: The rules and guidelines by which breeds are judged in dog shows.

Broken coat: An alternative name for wirehaired coats.

Canid: All members of the canine family.

Companion dogs: These dog breeds seem to have been kept for no purpose other than being good companions to their human masters. They include the Maltese, Chihuahua, Lhasa apso, shih tzu, Pekingese, pug, small poodle, dalmatian, cockapoo, and mixed-breed dogs.

Corkscrew: A term that describes a dog whose tail is twisted.

Coursing: A sport that evolved about two thousand years ago in which dogs run after hares.

Cur: A slang term used in describing a mixed-breed or homeless dog.

Doublecoat: Dogs with fur that has a resilient topcoat and a warmer, waterproof undercoat.

Draft dogs: While rare today, some larger breeds of dogs were once used to pull carts or power treadmills.

Feathering: A type of fur in which long fringe hairs on the legs and ears stick out.

Feral dog: A dog that lives independent of humans, never in a human home, but often close to them. They differ from stray dogs who, having been partially raised around or by humans, still tend to depend on them for food or periodic shelter.

Field trials: Agility tests for dogs, which might include things such as catching Frisbees and running obstacle courses.

Gait: The manner in which a dog walks or runs.

Gun dogs: As implied by the name, this particular category of dog often accompanies hunters because of their keen eyesight, sense of smell, and other abilities such as swimming. These dogs include standard poodles, retrievers, pointers, springer spaniels, cocker spaniels, Brittanies, and setters.

Hackles: Hairs that run down a dog's back that it raises when startled or otherwise challenged.

Hairlessness: An odd genetic rarity that breeders have tried to capture, but nearly all hairless breeds produce some pups with hair.

Harlequin: A fur pattern with splotches of black on white.

Heat: The female dog's fertile period (also called "coming into season").

Livestock dogs: A category of dogs bred to help with farming and livestock. They include German shepherds, border collies, Shetlands, sheepdogs, Welsh corgis, schnauzers, mountain dogs, wolfhounds, mastiffs, bulldogs, Great Danes, boxers, rottweilers, shar-peis, Newfoundlands, and St. Bernards.

Molossus: In ancient Rome this canine was used as a guardian and fierce killer. It is thought to have been a progenitor of the mastiff family.

Molt: The shedding of fur, usually associated with seasonal changes.

Opposite: Pieter Brueghel, Hunters in the Snow *(Kunsthistorisches Museum, Vienna).*

Mongrel: A dog that is the result of several mixed breedings (minimally two from two different types of dog).

Nana: The Newfoundland who appears in *Peter Pan* as a caretaker to and protector of the children.

Pack mentality: The tendencies of canines to travel together as a way of averting danger or for the purpose of hunting.

Pads: The cushioning on a dog's foot, just beneath the toes.

Pedigree: The lineage of an animal in recorded, traceable form.

Prick ear: An ear that is erect, similar to a bat ear except that it is pointed.

Primitive dogs: Dogs that trace their lineage to the Indian Plains wolf including the pharaoh hound, Ibizan hound, and Mexican hairless dog.

Random-bred dogs: Another way to describe a dog of questionable parentage. Because these dogs have not been routinely bred for specific traits, they usually suffer fewer genetic medical problems.

Saber tail: A dog's tail that is carried in a curve.

Scent hounds: A category of dogs that rely on their noses and endurance to corner prey. In this category are bassets, dobermans, bloodhounds, harriers, English foxhounds, coonhounds, water spaniels, and beagles.

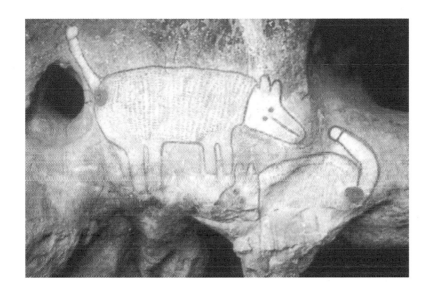

Cave painting of two dogs (Australia).

Scent marking: One of the ways that dogs communicate with each other and other animals is by scent marking. Dogs have marking glands on their tails, and when they brush them against an object, an aroma is left that marks territory.

Sensible breeding: Programs presently being put in place by many breeders to offset and correct the problems that stem from a lack of genetic diversity or carelessness in certain breeding programs, including a predisposition toward certain illnesses and physical deformity.

Setting: Stopping on command when game animals are sighted.

Sight hounds: A category of dogs who were bred for speed and characteristically have long legs and lean bodies. Included in this category we find greyhounds, wolfhounds, salukis, Afghans, and borzois.

Spritz dogs: A category of dogs that seem to have the closest affinity with humankind, and that characteristically have thick coats, strong muscles, and short ears. Included in this category are the Alaskan malamutes, chows, Akitas, keeshonds, Samoyeds, Siberian huskies, Pomeranians, and elkhounds.

Terriers: Originally a kind of hound, the terrier is aggressive, well muscled, hearty, and generally short-legged. Included in this category are fox terriers, Airedales, border terriers, cairn terriers, Scottish terriers, Yorkshires, pit bulls, Boston terriers, pinschers, schnauzers, and dachshunds.

Territorial tendency: Most dogs have this naturally—the desire to protect and guard their space. Exactly how actively a dog does this, and what constitutes "space" will vary according to the breed, upbringing, and the dog's training.

Topknot: Long fluffy hairs located on the top of a dog's head.

Tracker dogs: Canines with a natural ability for sniffing out a particular scent, often of people.

White Fang: A half-dog, half-wolf featured in a story by Jack London (1905).

BIBLIOGRAPHY

Ackroyd, Eric. *Dictionary of Dream Symbols.* London: Blandford Books, 1993.

Andrews, Ted. *Animal Speak.* St. Paul, Minn.: Llewellyn Publications, 1993.

Black, William George. *Folk Medicine.* New York: Burt Grankling Co., 1970.

Budge, E. A. Wallis. *Amulets & Superstitions.* Oxford: Oxford University Press, 1930.

Clark, Anne. *Beasts & Bawdy.* New York: Taplinger Publishing, 1975.

Cooper, J. C. *Symbolic and Mythological Animals.* London: Aquarian Press, 1992.

Cooper, Paulette and Paul Noble. *277 Secrets Your Dog Wants You to Know.* Berkley Calif.: Ten Speed Press, 1995.

Farrar, Janet and Stewart Farrar. *The Witches God.* Custer, Wash.: Phoenix Publishing, 1989.

————. *The Witches Goddess.* Custer Wash.: Phoenix Publishing, 1987.

Fogle, Bruce. *The Encyclopedia of the Dog.* New York: DK Publishing, 1995.

Fox Davies, A. C. *The Complete Guide to Heraldry.* New York: Crown Publishers, 1978.

Gonzalez-Wippler, Migene. *Amulets & Talismans.* St. Paul, Minn.: Llewellyn Publications, 1995.

Gordon, Stuart. *Encyclopedia of Myths & Legends.* London: Headline Books, 1993.

Gould, Charles. *Mythical Monsters.* New York: Crescent Books, 1989.

Hall, Manly P. *Secret Teachings of All Ages.* Los Angeles: Philosophical Research Society, 1977.

Hausman, Gerald and Loretta Hausman. *The Mythology of Dogs.* New York: St. Martin's Press, 1997.

Kieckhefer, Richard. *Magic in the Middle Ages.* Cambridge, England: Cambridge University Press, 1989.

Knappert, Jan. *African Mythology,* Wellingborough, England: Aquarian Press, 1990.

Kunz, George Frederick. *The Curious Lore of Precious Stones.* New York: Dover Publications, 1913.

Leach, Maria, ed. *Standard Dictionary of Folklore, Mythology, and Legend.* New York: HarperCollins, 1972.

Lorie, Peter. *Superstitions.* New York: Simon & Schuster, 1992.

Lum, Peter. *Fabulous Beasts.* New York: Pantheon Books, 1951.

Mery, Ferdnand. *The Life, History & Magic of the Dog.* New York: Grosset & Dunlap, 1968.

Miller, Gustavus. *Ten Thousand Dreams Interpreted.* Chicago: M. A. Donohue & Co., 1931.

Newall, Venetia. *Encyclopedia of Witchcraft & Magic.* New York: Dial Press, 1978.

Opie, Iona and Moria Tatem. *A Dictionary of Superstitions.* Oxford: Oxford University Press, 1990.

Sams, Jamie and David Carson. *Medicine Cards.* Santa Fe, N.M.: Bear & Co., 1988.

Steiger, Brad. *Totems.* San Francisco: Harper San Francisco, 1996.

Telesco, Patricia. *The Language of Dreams.* Freedom, Calif.: Crossing Press, 1997.

———. *Victorian Grimoire.* St. Paul, Minn.: Llewellyn Publications, 1992.

Thompson, C. J. S. *The Hand of Destiny.* New York: Bell Publishing Company, 1989.

Thurston, Mary Elizabeth. *The Lost History of the Canine Race.* Kansas City, Mo.: Andrews & McMeel, 1996.

Walker, Barbara. *The Woman's Dictionary of Symbols & Sacred Objects.* San Francico: Harper San Francisco, 1988.

Waring, Philippa. *The Dictionary of Omens & Superstitions.* Secaucus, N.J.: Chartwell Books, 1978.

White, T. H. *The Book of Beasts.* Mineola, N.Y.: Dover Publications, 1984.

Williams, Jude. *Jude's Herbal, Home Remedies.* St. Paul, Minn.: Llewellyn Publications, 1992.